CHILDREN
are like »»» ⟶
ARROWS
in the hands of a
WARRIOR

To my favorite Warriors, Continue to aim those Arrows. God has used you in such amazing ways! Love, Tammy

Helping Children Find Faith, Love, and Flight

TAMMY LARGIN

Selah Press PUBLISHING

CONTENTS

1. Our Release 1
2. Following the Master Warrior 3
3. The Needs of an Arrow 11
4. Gathering Materials for Our Quiver 27
5. Procuring Skills to Share 35
6. The Arrow's Shaft 45
7. Your Quiver 57
8. Choice...With Consequences 65
9. Straightening the Shaft 83
10. Inherited Skill 93
11. Preparing the Fletching 99
12. Crafting the Arrowhead 117
13. Arrow Assembly 125
14. Your Bow 145
15. Bowstring 151
16. Dressing for War 155
17. A Final Loving Warrior Warning 169
18. Time to Fly 173
19. From Quiver to HIS Target 177

"Your children are not your children.
They are sons and daughters of Life's longing for itself.
They come through you but not from you.
And though they are with you yet they belong not to you.

You may give them your love but not your thoughts,
For they have their own thoughts.
You may house their bodies but not their souls,
For thirsty souls dwell in the house of tomorrow,
which you cannot visit, not even in your dreams.
You may strive to be like them, but seek not to make them like you.
For life goes not backward nor tarries with yesterday.
You are the bows from which your children as living arrows are sent forth.

The archer sees the make upon the path of the infinite, and He bends you with His might that His arrows may go swift and far.
Let your bending in the archer's hand be for gladness.
For even as He loves the arrow that flies, so He also loves the bow that is stable."

Kahlil Gibran (Christian Philosopher)

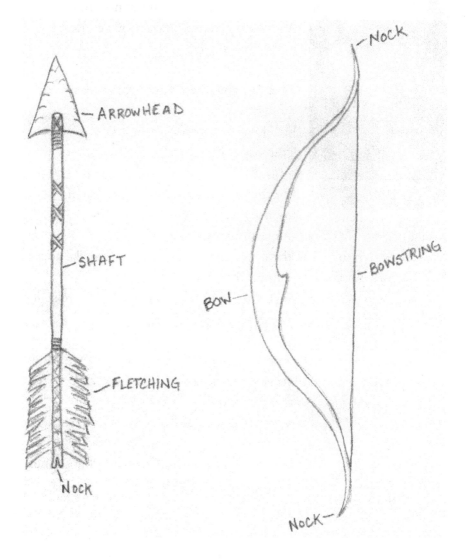

ARROWHEAD

SHAFT

FLETCHING

NOCK

NOCK

BOW

BOWSTRING

NOCK

Chapter One

>>>————————————————→

OUR RELEASE

On August 23, 2018, with a backpack in hand, I grabbed the bow. My daughter, the arrow, was already in the car. As we ran out, I turned to face the front door, pulling hard to close it tight. Pushing the lock button on the handle made my decision final. I jumped in the car. My husband and I looked at the clock—it was 5:15 a.m. We knew there was a deadline. We had to be ready to shoot at 6:18 a.m. If we missed our shot, she'd miss the target. The seventeen years of training seemed very short—too short. Had we completely prepped our arrow? Was the arrow straight? Did I comb the feathers tight? Should we sharpen the head just a little more before we arrive? These questions were going through my mind over and over again.

We drove for forty-five minutes to get to our location. When we arrived, we pulled the backpack from the car and carefully placed it on the arrow. Then we prepared to take the shot. I remember clipping the arrow into the bow string. It was so tight. I fought with the string, not sure if I was going to get it clipped in. My emotions ran high, and as I began to draw back from the bow, I struggled to get it to full extension. *I'm not strong enough for this*, I thought. *The string is just too tight.* I felt my cheeks begin to heat up, and the tears began to fill my eyes. I couldn't do it by myself. I kept trying to pull back, but then I remembered, *This was a couple's shot.* I wasn't supposed to do it by myself. My husband was there to help me, and he stood behind me with his body spooning close—his arms around mine. Our left hands on the bow, our right holding the arrow clipped into the string. We both began to pull. We raised the bow to the sky and pulled with everything we had. Finally, the bow was at full extension. We lowered the bow, putting the target in our sight. The target was 4,360 miles away, and it was time to release.

As we let go, she began to fly, and our tears began to fall. They weren't tears of total sadness, but tears of accomplishment, pride, and joy—all at the same time. My husband and I closed our eyes and took a deep breath. The peace of God entered as we inhaled. We held our breath for a moment, then slowly we exhaled and opened our eyes. The sky was still dark, but we saw her light shaped like an arrow soaring over the Atlantic to Praia on the island of Santiago, Cape Verde, Africa, headed for God's target.

Chapter Two

FOLLOWING THE MASTER WARRIOR

The LORD continued, "Look, stand near me on this
rock. As my glorious presence passes by, I will hide
you in the crevice of the rock and cover you with my
hand until I have passed by"
(Exodus 33:21–22 NLT).

Going to the mountains is a return to home for me. They don't need
to be the same mountains I grew up in; they can be any mountains. A
couple weeks out of the summer, I go up into the north Georgia
Appalachian Mountains to teach horse camp. At night as I camp alone,
looking up at the beautiful canvas of stars on a black sky, that teenage
girl of my youth returns, and I am reminded that life is about the
journey—God's journey. As I absorb the beauty of God's creation, the
wind blows gently on my face, and I feel as if God's glory passes by. It
is as if He is covering my eyes as He passes, breathing on me the peace
that surpasses all understanding.

This peace is what I felt the moment I found out I was pregnant.
After months of trying, I had decided to just let go, and God distracted
me. Then without my knowledge, He heard my prayer, breathed on
me, and brought life to my womb.

He didn't only breathe on me, but God has breathed on all
humans, creating their lives from the beginning, just as He says in His
Word:

> Then the LORD God formed a man from the dust of
> the ground and breathed into his nostrils the breath of
> life, and the man became a living being (Genesis 2:7
> NIV).

Speaking of the breath of God, I heard a great sermon on this topic by Joby Martin, founder and lead pastor of The Church of Eleven22 in Jacksonville, Florida. Joby talked about how God was physically face to face with Adam when God blew breath into Adam. I could picture the scene: Adam was lying on the dirt, arms by his side, lifeless, yet in full form. God could have used His hands and given the motion for Adam to "rise up." God could have just said with a commanding voice, "Come to LIFE!" But He didn't. God wanted His face to be the only thing that Adam saw when he opened his eyes for the first time. God wanted Adam to know that he was known. I can imagine God on His hands and knees at the head of Adam, face to face, and God breathing. The Hebrew word for "breath" literally means nostril to nostril. God didn't just blow, He inflated Adam's lungs with His breath nostril to nostril. And when Adam opened his eyes the face of God was all he saw—no trees, no sky, no sun—just the face of his creator.[1]

Because of this face-to-face moment and the feeling of being known, Adam had chosen to trust God, who, in turn, gave Adam a tour of what had been created especially for him. Flowers of every shape and size abounded with such vivid color that Adam felt the need to touch them to see if they were real. Sounds of birds and animals played like a symphony of instrumentation, and fruits had such a sweet, strong aroma that Adam could almost taste them before he put them in his mouth. Everything was plentiful.

As soon as we found out we were going to be parents, my husband, Bill, and I thought: *If the Lord God formed a man from the dust of the ground (as Genesis 2:7 says), shouldn't He be the foremost influencer when it comes to rearing a child?* This belief led us on a quest to intentionally raise our daughter with a focus on God's Word, rather than on the world's influencers. This biblical parenting journey would not have been successful without a relationship with Jesus Christ. Because of our relationship with Him, we knew that we would be called to be stewards and warriors for our child—who would also be a beautiful creation made by God. Also, because we knew our Creator is the Master Warrior, and we knew that if we were teachable, He would teach us everything we needed to know. He would enable us to be stewards as well as warriors, who could train and equip the little "arrow" He had just created in my womb. He would train us according to His instruction manual, which was also written by His very breath, as we see in the following verse:

> All Scripture is God-breathed and is useful for teaching, rebuking, correcting and training in righteousness, so that the servant of God may be thoroughly equipped for every good work (2 Timothy 3:16–17 NIV).

Warrior Training

Yes, my fellow parents, as you likely know, this training is for us, too. To be one of His warriors that will someday launch His new arrow, He is giving us the privilege of learning from Him. My husband and I learned that our classroom is His creation, our textbook is the Bible, and our professor is Jesus Christ our Lord and Savior. All we need to bring is gratitude for this honor of stewarding His creation and a teachable heart. Now that my arrow is launched, I couldn't be more grateful for the times I followed Him, and for the privilege of being used as this steward. However, in the trenches of parenthood, I remember how hard it was to follow His training!

And then, at the same time as we are in training, we have to fight the weapons thrown at us from the world. The world's goal for our children is to get them to conform to various pressures at the expense of their individuality. But God's goal for our children is for them to be grounded in their identity in Him so strongly that they confidently use and express that individuality so much that people see that difference in their lives, thereby glorifying Him—not the world.

My heart in writing this book is to give those of you who are somewhere on the parenthood journey a training manual to help you both hear God's lessons and fight the all-too-frequent attacks from the world. I am so grateful that He breathed both these spiritual lessons and practical tips into my heart as His warrior! I consider them gifts from my Heavenly Father! Part of the stewardship journey for me has been to pass along these gifts verbally as others have asked through the years. By His grace, He has enabled me to compile them in writing, using a framework based on archery, which has recently become dear to my heart.

So, warriors in training, are you ready to begin your training? I hope so! If not, I know parenthood and life is busy, but I strongly encourage you to begin as soon as you can! Your arrow will be the desired age of launch faster than you think—any parent with kids older than eighteen will attest to that!!

Yay! I'm so glad you have chosen to go on this journey with me! I know God will honor your commitment and your effort!

Let's start with a closer look at the target, along with what my husband and I call the key passage of scripture for this journey.

Before I move on, I want to point out that at the end of Chapter One, my husband and I didn't refer to the target as "our target" or "our daughter's target," but instead, we referred to it as "God's target." The end goal to remember is that although we are to influence and train, we do not get to choose where our children will land. We are given the gift of a child to "Train up…in the way he should go [teaching him to seek God's wisdom and will for his abilities and talents], Even when he is old he will not depart from it" (Proverbs 22:6 AMP).

I also want to point out that the Master Warrior set our course—I don't believe any warriors can succeed on this training journey well without Him. Following His training as we learn is paramount. With all that said, let's learn more about what training means.

The Hebrew word for "train up" in this verse is hanak. "Dedicate" is the English translation. Check out Webster's definitions:

1. to devote to the worship of a divine being
2. specifically: to set apart (a church) to sacred uses with solemn rites
3. to set apart to a definite use
4. to commit to a goal or way of life
5. to inscribe or address by way of compliment
6. to open to public use [1]

My thoughts were expanded when I read these definitions. They describe part of the path that parents would be wise to follow to rear God-fearing children. In the section that follows, I'll show you how each definition of "dedicate" corresponds to biblical guidance for parenthood.

- Definition number one corresponds with a verse in Romans, which tells us that we are to guide, not cling to our children, thereby giving each child as a "living and holy sacrifice acceptable to God which is our spiritual service of worship" (Romans 12:1).
- Definition number two shows that we are to be comfortable with the skin God gave our children. Having them be set apart sets them up to be used positively for the future of God's kingdom.
- Definition number three speaks of two parts: committing to a goal and a way of life. This goal is the one God has for them, not a goal that we as parents have for them. Parents also need to be an example so children can see the blessings of living His way of life.
- Definition number four describes our job as one that inscribes or addresses with a compliment. This action comes by encouraging our children in their strengths and gifts, complimenting more than criticizing, and recognizing the good versus the bad in all choices as lessons learned.

- And then definition number five, the real kicker, is that our children have to be ready to share their testimonies with the public. Hopefully, as parents we have helped them see their testimonies and the blessings of God along the way.

A Prayer as We Begin

Father God, I lift up these new warriors reading this book and learning about each part of the analogy in parenting represented by the arrow, bow, armor, and releasing toward Your target. May each of them take the time to sit back, take a deep breath, and allow You to give them Your solutions to help their families create community, love, and graciousness for one another. May they not just take advice from my husband's and my journey, because we know, Father, that no two families are alike. Thank you that You give each of us ideas to help spur others on as they hear Your ideas for their families. I pray that each warrior reading this book would find the grace to think out of the box and to keep their eyes on you, God, as You prepare them to release each of Your arrows toward Your targets. In Jesus name, Amen (Let it be so).

A Fundamental Invitation for Some

If any of you do not have a relationship with Jesus Christ, I invite you to go to the prayer in the back of this book (page 181) to begin a relationship with Him that will help you live a life of hope and joy. A relationship with Christ is the foundation of everything I teach in this book. If you accept Christ, the Holy Spirit will help you understand more about the biblical principles discussed. If you make that decision, I am confident that you will also feel the breeze of His glory as you begin to know Him and seek Him through this journey of stewarding your arrow.

Takeaway Transformation Tips for Parenting Our Arrows

This section, found at the end of each chapter, reiterates key points that you can refer to again and again. I would also love it if you would share these tips on social media to help others who may want pointers on the biblical parenting journey. If you use the hashtag provided, I'll be able to see your posts and interact with you!

- Encouraging our children in their strengths and gifts, complimenting more than criticizing, and recognizing the good versus the bad in all choices as lessons learned. #helpthemfindlove

CHILDREN ARE LIKE ARROWS IN THE HANDS OF A WARRIOR

Chapter Three

THE NEEDS OF
AN ARROW

What marvelous love the Father has extended to us!
Just look at it—we're called children of God! That's
who we really are. But that's also why the world
doesn't recognize us or take us seriously, because it
has no idea who he is or what he's up to
(1 John 3:1 MSG).

The marvelous love God has given to us is one of unconditional love. He loves us so much that He calls us His children. He loves us no matter what we have done in the past, because what He created us to do for His purpose is not dependent on our previous actions. He loves us just because He created us. Following His example, we are to have unconditional love for our children, and this love is to begin at conception. Most mothers love and begin to know a child long before she ever holds her child in her arms. That's why if a mother miscarries a child the grief is so great. When parents know and love their children, and if they follow God's example of training their arrows that we talked about in the last chapter, they will also challenge their warriors in the ways that God directs. Meeting these three needs—to be known, to be loved, and to be challenged—helps our children grow into well-balanced adults.

Unfortunately, as the verse we just read says, much of the world doesn't know God or understand God's love because the enemy perpetually tries to influence the world and our children. Our Master

Warrior, however, equips us for the task of training our arrows for the battle ahead by enabling us to meet these needs.

As we take the next step in training our arrows, let's take a closer look at these foundational needs and how God equips us to meet them. We'll also examine some of the enemy's common ploys and how God enables us to overcome these schemes. We will then keep learning about God's strategies and how He is equipping us to be His stewards of our arrows.

To Be Known

Let's review a verse from Genesis that we looked at in the last chapter as we explore how we can express to our children that they are known.

> The LORD God formed a man from the dust of the ground and breathed into his nostrils the breath of life, and the man became a living being (Genesis 2:7 NIV).

Just like Adam, our children are known first by God as they are exposed to His breath when He creates them. With our children, God included us in the process of creating them and loving them as parents. **Adam was shown that he was known** by God from the moment he was awakened by the close proximity he had with his Creator. Like God, parents will be the first ones to see their future arrows when they are born. Like Adam, our arrows need eye-to-eye contact with their caring warriors.

Many midwives also believe it is important to have skin-to-skin contact immediately with our newborns. The touch of skin enables them to hear the familiar heartbeat, which they also heard in the womb. This contact provides the first opportunity for them to feel known by us, their parents, in a world that wants to distract and move their focus from the One who knows all of us the best, the Master Warrior and Creator, God. In 1 John 4:7, God calls us "Beloved," but if God calls us His Beloved, how can Satan have access to the most important of these key needs?

The answer is described in Genesis 3. If you have never read this portion of God's Word, I suggest you do so. In this chapter, we see that the reason the enemy has had access to humans is because Adam and Eve became visually impaired by Satan and forgot who knew them best—their Father. Eve became distracted, and lost sight of the fact that they were known by the Master Warrior. She let the words of someone else cloud her thoughts. Adam too, lost sight of his Father, when he also chose to eat the fruit from the tree of the knowledge of good and evil. Their shame made them hide from their Father and their sin built a wall that separated Adam's family from God. This separation opened the door for the enemy to wage war against us because Adam took the authority God had given him and handed it over to Satan. With Jesus, God provided a remedy to reconcile people back to a relationship with Himself, but the enemy still tries to wage war against us—even though he has been defeated through the blood of Jesus' death on the cross. Don't let Satan distract you from the stewardship of your arrows! Help them feel known. But how do I do that you ask? From day one, be intentional and make time daily to spend with your arrows.

I knew a battle was being waged from the moment I conceived—even before that. It had taken months to get pregnant. Because I was thirty-six years old, the doctors deemed that I had a "risky pregnancy." Above thirty-five, many doctors require additional testing, but Bill and I declined the tests for birth defects. We put our trust in God that this child would be who He chose for us. We didn't even want to know the gender. There are so few surprises in the world, and this one, to us, would be the best.

As far as pregnancy goes, mine was pretty uneventful. I didn't have morning sickness (definitely a blessing), and I got plenty of sleep. But as I rounded my fifth month, I had a sharp, single stab of pain that took me to the floor. I was in the middle of teaching second grade for summer school, when suddenly, my legs buckled under the pain of a stab to my right side. The pain lasted for just a second, but my principal came running, and she took over my class as I drove quickly to the emergency room at the women's hospital at the demand of my doctor. Bill met me there. Ultrasounds, urinalysis, and blood work all came back clear. But the event planted a seed that something was not right. Still, we clung to God's promise that we would have this child, and in exchange, this child would be dedicated to God. Satan had tried to thwart the pregnancy—but God had a greater plan.

As warriors in training, we need to understand that Satan has a plan for every child a mother carries. If he can't stop a child from being born, his next plan usually focuses on stealing a child's identity—to try to keep that child from feeling truly known. Satan is not shy, as you can see if you look at the passage where he tempts Jesus. "**If** you are the Son of God…" (Matthew 4:3 NIV, bold added for emphasis). He even attacks the Son of God's identity. Satan is waiting to attack every child both in the womb and out.

When we face attacks from the enemy, whether before our birth or at any age, all of us need to remember that being a child of God is our identity. The Bible affirms our creation when it says, "So God created human beings in his own image. In the image of God he created them; male and female he created them" (Genesis 1:27 NLT). Notice how this sentence reminds us three times that God is our Creator, not Satan, which means His plan can start at conception. How is it that Satan continues to try and steal our identity when God repeats Himself three times in this passage?

The battle for identity never stops. Every day as warriors, we have to choose Christ as our identity, and we have to remind ourselves that we are known by God. As stewards of our arrows, we are called to our knees to pray for our arrows that the Holy Spirit will place a protective hedge around them. We will help lay a foundation of identity for them based in God's Word as we help them understand the truth found there. Daily, remind your arrows that they have been called by name and they belong to the Master Warrior.

But now thus says the LORD, he who created you, O Jacob, he who formed you, O Israel: "Fear not, for I have redeemed you; I have called you by name, you are mine" (Isaiah 43:1 ESV).

Many Christians believe that the names we give our children are actually written in Heaven before they arrive in our arms. We see examples of God giving names to parents in Luke 1, when the angel Gabriel appeared before Zechariah to say that his older wife will have a son and his name is to be John, which means Jehovah is a gracious giver. In Matthew 1:20–21 an angel appears to Joseph and tells him that he is to name Mary's baby, Jesus, which means Jehovah is salvation. God knows us before we arrive on Earth as He tells us in His Word: "Before I formed you in the womb, I knew you; Before you were born I sanctified you; I ordained you a prophet to the nations" (Jeremiah 1:5 NKJV). I believe if we seek Him, God will reveal our children's names to us, and I think He uses those names to help us begin to know our children from the moment we know we have conceived.

From the moment we name our babies, we begin to say their names (sometimes even when they are still in the womb). Within hours of birth, they begin to acknowledge their parents through stares as they learn to focus on their faces. As they begin to grow and their neck muscles strengthen, they begin to turn their heads to make eye contact with the voices speaking to them. As parents, we rock and sing their names, repeating them over and over as if we are training the babies to hear our voices as voices of security and safety. We may also sing a comforting song to soothe their tears.

Lilly was our little sunshine, and whenever she was upset or scared, I would sing "You Are My Sunshine" quietly in her ear and her tears would subside. Her hearing my familiar voice would help satisfy one of her greatest needs: being known.

You will hear people say over and over that time is short, so hold and enjoy your little arrow as you continue to show that you plan to know everything about them. As they talk, share in the conversation even if you can't translate their language yet. Listening intently as if you are interested in every word shows that you are working to know who God is preparing them to be. Once they begin walking, walk beside them teaching them about their surroundings through nature and find your inner child as you learn about THEIR world as your NEW world. I began to see things from knee height and God used that to make me more aware of how He sees all aspects of life, not just what we see at eye level. Don't be exasperated by the "why" questions. If you don't know the answer, say you don't know, then use those moments to learn together. Only give them enough information at a time to answer the question. Your kids don't want the encyclopedia version; they want the Children's Reader's Digest version. By answering questions as they ask, you will get to know your arrow better than anyone else. Then reverse the role as you see them mature. It is now your turn to ask the questions. God does this role reversal so you can HELP them maneuver life in the future, not dictate a life for their future. Doing these things helps your child consistently know they are known.

Also, don't let those who do not know God and His purpose for their lives influence your child's identity or what they think about themselves. If children don't feel known by parents, they will seek to figure out their identity elsewhere like school, friends, and social media.

How do we get back to family first so that our kids feel known by us to help guard them from wanting to only be known and liked by the world? We as warriors, have to be intentional with our children and how we prepare our arrows for this world. God has everything we need in His Word, but we must spend time in the Bible to find it. We must listen to the wise counsel that God has put in our paths, and we must tune into the Holy Spirit when plans or comments from friends or family don't settle well with us.

A different version of our key verse that we looked at in the last chapter says, "Train up a child in the way he should go [teaching him to seek God's wisdom and will for his abilities and talents], Even when he is old he will not depart from it" (Proverbs 22:6 AMP). This verse reaffirmed that God's Word is the foundation of truth, and with it comes God's wisdom. God and His Word is our influencer. The hard part is turning off the voices of this world.

To do our best to prevent the tragedies of this world, like addiction and suicide, we have to remind our children that the only true place of safety is being known, and where they can be best known is in the arms of Jesus. Make your home His home. We have prayed over and anointed with oil the threshold of our home to make sure demons know that Jesus lives here. When demons see Him, they flee, and our children are kept safe from evil. In Psalms 23:5 it says, "You prepare a table before me in the presence of my enemies; you have anointed my head with oil; my cup overflows." God prepares a table for us in front of our enemies, and He anoints us with oil to protect our minds. As Christians, many of us use oil to anoint our homes, protecting our families from demons, and evil. Demons don't want to be around Jesus. In some instances, my husband and I have seen people we have invited in actually stand outside the door of our house and even take a step backward. I don't know if these people have a demon operating in them or not, but we always know the Lord is protecting us since we have anointed our home with His protection.

Whenever I need to feel known and therefore safe with God, I find myself singing the words to my favorite song, "The More I Seek You," by Kari Jobe, which you can listen to by holding the camera on your phone over the following QR code:

I learned this song just a couple years after Lilly was born, and I knew that the words describe my safe place. I wanted Lilly to know that we are her safe place here on Earth. I want her to know that she is known the way this song makes me feel known. Like David, the Great King in the Bible, we also wanted her to know...

The God! His way is perfect;
The promise of HASHEM is flawless,
He is a shield for all who take refuge in Him (Psalm 18:31
Tanach).

To Be Loved

There are so many parts of…to be loved. For some, love is provision, a roof over our heads, food in our belly, and toys to play with, but those are just byproducts of love. Love is so much more. As parents, love is stopping in the middle of what you are doing, no matter how important, and listening to what your child needs to say to you at that moment in time. Love is waking up in the middle of the night to sing a sick child to sleep and then schlepping to the bathroom to clean up the mess. Love is knowing that it doesn't matter what you accomplish in this world as long as you—a warrior in God still in training of your own—are preparing your children—future warriors in training—to first be an arrow ready for battle. Being entrusted with a child is the most important gift you will ever receive from God because it is a gift of purpose.

Love is sacrifice. In John 3:16 we see "God gave his only Son…" This example shows us how God wants us to be able to release our children. Our children will hopefully not have to hang on a cross like Jesus did. And unless we have lost a child, or we have watched a child suffer in immense pain, I'm not sure we can even begin to fathom the excruciating pain God must have endured to put Jesus through the crucifixion so that our sins can be forgiven. Christ also made the final choice to die for our sins—God did not force Him. God calls us to remember that choice, and as stewards of our children, we need to step back and allow them to choose to go wherever they feel God has called them. In obedience, we then surrender our children's lives at present and in the future as a form of worship, being thankful for the opportunity to train up a warrior of God.

Daily, as we were raising Lilly, we would give Lilly to God knowing that we would make mistakes, misdirect her, and give her worldly advice over His Word. We are far from perfect, and we have failed multiple times at most of what I share with you in this book. But the times we got it right and listened to God's direction, He blessed us and put our family back on the right path.

God gave us children to help us wake up to what is really important in life. We learned that what was valuable to us was not going into debt for that new car or buying a house that is beyond our financial means. Those fancy, expensive clothes and that $7 cup of coffee aren't what's really important either. What's most important is investing your time and resources in your family. As I raised Lilly, I often thought back to one of the greatest gifts ever—a small piece of relevant advice from my mom. She said, "Don't worry about cleaning the house. Your child is only with you for a short time, so just savor every moment." For most of us, if the average age of death is seventy-three, that means you will have a child living at home for only twenty-five percent of your lifespan.

For me, what was important was my calling to focus on God so I could be obedient in raising Lilly. All relationships come from God, but if your priority is a good relationship with your child over God you will never win. Instead, the voices of this world will win. I needed to know that when Lilly is called to her kingdom job and leaves home, I will have loved her with a contagious love that she will carry with her. The love instilled in her will draw others to her to know Jesus, and then later, this love will allow her to love her own children with that same kind of love. 1 John 4:19 says, "We love because He first loved us."

God's love is overflowing, and I have experienced His love, which surpasses all understanding. Even though I served God on the mission field in my teen years, in my twenties I ran away from Him, ashamed of whom I had become. In the midst of my loneliness and sorrow, a worshipper in a little church bellowed "Just As I Am."

> Just as I am without one plea
> But that thy blood was shed for me
> And as thou bidst me come to thee
> Oh Lamb of God I come, I come.

When I heard that familiar song, He drew me to Himself, and He used His saints to pray with me. In that scene, He reached down and saved me from the darkest pit of self-loathing and brought me into His marvelous light. This overflowing love, His love, of Him meeting me right where I was is how I want to love my Lilly. I want to love her without judgement or condemnation; I only want to pour out unconditional love.

Loving our children the way Christ loves them—where they are at—is especially important to counter the world's messages, which tell them that they must change to be loved. Our children aren't the only ones being targeted. The world's messages tell all of us that we are the most imperfect of creatures. We are too fat…too tall…too short. We have the wrong hair color…we need Botox…we need more exercise—the list is never-ending. But none of these messages are what God says. He created us, and He wants to show each of us what He sees in us as individuals. To help us believe what God says about us instead of what the world says about us, we would be wise to continue to absorb truth from what His Word has to say to us. A couple key truths include, We "are fearfully and wonderfully made," (Psalm 139:14 NIV) and we are God's "workmanship, created in Christ to do good works" (Ephesians 2:10 NIV). We would also be wise to instill these loving messages into our children's lives to combat the lies of the world.

Part of instilling these truths into our children's lives is by observing how God loves people and by learning from Him as we go about our own day-to-day lives. I got a unique opportunity to see what God saw in a group of kids several years ago when I was working with deaf young adults. It was not an easy job. Many of them did not grow up in Christian homes, and they felt they were entitled to more because of their inability to hear. My job was to show them that they were as capable as anyone else of doing the occupations of their dreams if they put sweat and tears into learning. One of the things I loved most about working with the deaf community is that I knew where I stood with them. Their feelings showed in the signs students gave me for my name. Those students I taught who disliked me gave me sign names that were sometimes embarrassing; those who were acquaintances tended to give sign names that described physical appearance, and those who loved me, gave me sign names placed over their heart, which is how love for someone would be conveyed in sign language.

Similar to many of the affectionate sign names given to me by the deaf community, giving your children nicknames shows that you have a love for him/her that goes beyond what the world would initially see in them. I encourage you to therefore use uplifting and supportive nick names that inspire your children to adopt positive characteristics and confidence. I'd also recommend asking God what He sees reflected in your child as you consider a nickname. Perhaps you will find a word that means something to only you and your child. To her father and me, Lilly is beautiful, so that is her nickname. I call her "Beautiful" when I address her in person and in writing. The definition of "beautiful" is learned early when children are young, and whatever Lilly sees as beautiful, my hope is that it reminds her that she embodies that word.

To Be Challenged

We do not know the age of Adam when God created him, but God had prepared a purpose or a job for Adam from the very beginning to challenge him. Adam is told his purpose in Genesis 2:15, which is to "...dress and keep" the garden of Eden. Similarly, God has a purpose or job for each of our children, in which He will challenge them and invite us into the process of preparing them for that challenge. Sometimes, God uses unique abilities to show us and our kids that they are overcomers and capable of meeting the challenges with our help.

Lilly was born with a unique ability. She has a banded right hand, which means she has a palm but no fingers, and half of a thumb, which looks like a toe. When Lilly was a toddler, she would do almost everything with her banded right hand between her thumb and palm. She picked up Cheerios, green beans, or anything else she ate with her right hand, which meant neurologically she was right-handed.

Lilly's first big challenge came when she was about eighteen months old. She would sit in her highchair and want to scribble on paper. First, we bought the large crayons without thinking about her little "fin" of a hand. She tried to grab the large crayon, but it didn't fit. I went to my craft closet and grabbed regular crayons. They had a better fit, but they didn't last. Lilly would begin to color, and the crayon would break. She would throw that crayon over her shoulder, grab another crayon, and it too would break. This cycle would go on for about four or five crayons until we could see she was mad. She would wrinkle her nose, take a deep breath, then breathe it out through her teeth, spraying everything with spit in her path as we tried not to laugh. Eventually, we just had broken crayons that she found to actually work perfectly in her hand since they were too short to break. She had found the resolution to her first big challenge.

Having a banded hand meant many challenges for Lilly, and much "stand back and watch torture" for us. No parents like to see their child struggle, but it is through the struggle that God grows us, so this difficulty was part of both our growth and her growth as well. She accomplished much by the age of three: dressing herself, playing with various toys, and riding a scooter. My favorite challenge happened when Lilly was also around three years old. I took her with me when I flew to Texas to spend some time with my cousin Angela and her daughter, Taylor. Taylor is only twenty months older than Lilly, and they enjoyed one another's company. Angela and I wanted a night out by ourselves, so Angela made reservations for the girls at Taylor's gym at a Parent's Night Out program. We dropped them off and went out for a nice dinner and a movie, but the real show happened when we returned to the gym. When we asked for the girls, the guy at the counter said, "Oh, you are Lilly's mom, come with me. She wanted to show you something when you got here." I followed him through the gym, and he called out to her. We stopped at the uneven bars. He pulled out the bounce board and placed it under the bar. Lilly held the bar with her left hand, palm away and then placed her right wrist, palm toward her on the bar. Bouncing on the board, she pulled herself up. Then with little help, she did a hip circle around the bar and popped off. WOW! *What just happened?* The guy from the gym told me he had never seen anyone so determined to get onto the bar. He said she spent the better part of that night figuring out what would work for her little hand. I was glad I wasn't there. I would have been trying to work out the problem for her, and because I wasn't, she stepped up to the challenge. And since we were in Texas at the time, let's just say she took the bull by the horns.

Challenging our kids can be hard. Many of us claim that allowing our children to participate in certain activities at home takes more time to teach than to do it ourselves. The problem with this belief is, if you don't let them try, how will they learn to apply the knowledge they have to solve problems on their own? In the old days, we called this ability to apply knowledge to new situations common sense.

Much of my common sense came from the opportunity I had to work beside my parents beginning at age ten. They bought a guest ranch in Colorado. My favorite place to hang out on the ranch was the roof of the old Lake House cabin. From there, I could see Mount Nast towering among a cluster of mountains in the Colorado Rockies. I could also see Nast Lake, where I caught dozens of rainbow trout as a child. The storms rolling in from the valley brought the cool, fresh scent of rain. If I close my eyes today, I can still feel the wind gently blowing my hair back across my face. On that roof, all alone, I knew I was known and loved by my Creator, and I knew the opportunity to work at the ranch was my challenge.

My parents had chosen to purchase the guest ranch because they wanted us to have an experience like no other. They wanted us to be in a place where they would not only rear us with people who visited from around the world, but also, they wanted us to have the chance to participate in their work with them if we chose to do so. My mornings began bright and early at 6 a.m. My first job was to get the coffee pot brewing for fifty guests and workers, who would be walking in at various times until breakfast at 8 a.m. Then it was off to the barn to feed forty horses sweet feed and hay with the cowboys. I would rush back to the lodge just in time for breakfast to be hot and ready to serve the people at the tables. Each day could bring a different adventure. There were trail rides, jeep trips, and rafting on the Roaring Fork River. Other activities that I helped out with included square dancing and singing, watching movies and the Friday night hayride. My responsibilities grew each year until I could almost run the place myself, but I loved working with my parents up until I was twenty-one, when my dad sold the ranch.

My parents took the time to teach me each aspect of the ranch so that I understood that many jobs are connected. The process of cooking a meal for fifty was math and science as well as taste. Caring for animals also helped us learn how to care for people. My dad taught me that everything was a production line, and the organization of my process determined the speed of my accomplishment. I always appreciated that my parents didn't think my age was a factor of my ability to accomplish what was put before me. It was simply my challenge to overcome.

My dad was also up front about the feast and famine approach to entrepreneurship. We learned how to shop wisely in bulk, to buy when items were on sale, and to live without our wants, knowing that it was wise to fulfill only our needs until the feast returned. He made sure we saw that adulting was tough but satisfying. Like arrows in his quiver, we were with my dad as he included us in both the work and the rewards. He knew that it was not wise to hide the stresses of everyday life from us. If we didn't see difficulties growing up, how were we going to learn to face them head on and not skirt the problems Satan throws our way?

My husband, Bill, like me, had family members teach him valuable lessons. His grandparents invited him each summer to live with them at their lake house in rural north Georgia. Bill worked side by side with his Poppi to maintain the property, and he helped with the maintenance of their lake house and boat. His Poppi challenged his mind by teaching him new skills like using a chainsaw, fixing a boat motor, and driving a car, which helped him develop problem-solving capabilities that he would carry into adulthood.

Our parents prepared us as their arrows by offering us challenges in the mountains and at the lake, and our experiences allowed us to fly with all the skills necessary for life, no matter where we went. Bill's grandparents took the time to show him love and teach him while his parents provided for the family. Not all of us can buy a guest ranch or a lake house to help teach our children, but we can involve them in the life we are currently living.

At a couple points in Lilly's childhood, Bill lost his job for long stretches of time. When Lilly was two, he was jobless for two years, and when she was five, he was out of work for almost three years. Our family had to learn to cut expenses, to survive on savings, and to work odd jobs for friends with Lilly at our side. Just like my dad did with me, we were frank with Lilly and included Lilly in the search for good deals and free ideas. We would scour the stores for red or yellow clearance stickers, which Lilly could identify. She loved our cheap treats: buy-one, get-one-free shakes at Steak–n-Shake or Sonic. We would check the Internet to find new parks and invite friends to join us there to save money rather than going to restaurants. Allowing her to participate in money-saving activities gave her a chance to feel known, loved, and challenged.

Encourage your kids to join you in every venture whether you are planting a garden, cleaning the house, or going to your job as a mechanic. All you have to do is share the skills needed to be good at the task. You never know if God will be using that skill to help them feel known, loved, or challenged.

Takeaway Transformation Tips for Parenting Our Arrows

- Meeting these three needs—to be known, to be loved, and to be challenged—helps our children grow into well-balanced adults. #helpthembecomeawarrior
- In obedience, we then surrender our children's lives at present and in the future as a form of worship, being thankful for the opportunity to train up a warrior of God. #helpthemfindflight
- If we didn't see difficulties growing up, how were we going to learn to face them head on and not skirt the problems Satan throws our way? #helpthemfindflight

Chapter Four

GATHERING THE MATERIALS
FOR OUR QUIVERS

*Like arrows in the hands of a warrior are children
born in one's youth. Blessed is the man whose quiver
is full of them. They will not be put to shame when
they contend with their opponents in court
(Psalm 127:4–5 NIV).*

During biblical times an arrow had two purposes: killing animals for food and fighting in warfare. With the advent of technology, we no longer have to hunt for meals, but we do still have to fight the war between good and evil. Therefore, as I've shared, our children need to be trained up to be arrows, crafted through the hands of the Master Warrior and trained by parent warriors who are themselves being trained through the guidance of the Holy Spirit.

Moving forward, I'll share my understanding about the parts of the arrow and its craftsmanship as an analogy for our parenting journeys. Learning how to create an arrow, a technical process, may take years to understand, just as parenting can. The good news is that God guides us through the process of raising and eventually shooting our arrows at God's targets.

The process of traditional arrow making is almost a lost art. Inventions like fiberglass make arrows lighter than they once were. In modern day, machines do the balancing, and lasers make the arrows straight with consistency. This method makes it easier for the arrows to be created almost perfectly. Before these inventions, the original process to make arrows was painstaking. Traditionally, arrows were made by the warrior that would use them. An arrow made quickly without careful intentionality could cause it to miss an important target such as an animal or an enemy. Therefore, the craftsmanship that went into making each arrow was a matter of life and death. The journey that a warrior takes while making the arrow is one that will, if done with precision, ensure it hits the target. If you want to be a warrior in training for yourself, your child, or future children, the first step is to gather your materials with a keen eye.

Imagine that you are indeed a warrior, and you don't have the modern technologies that you need to make an arrow. What would you do instead? You would walk through the field of reeds or saplings where you would carefully pick through the bushes and trees to find a straight piece of wood that was close to the diameter you wanted for the arrow. Then you would test the bend of the raw wood to make sure it was strong enough to take the penetration of flesh. If there is too much bend, the wood might dry crooked. If there is not enough bend, the wood could become brittle during the drying process. Suffice it to say that without the foundation of a good wood shaft, you cannot make a good arrow.

Considering the traditional making of an arrow reminds me of when I was pregnant. I would peruse books and videos about what to expect. Countless hours of dates with Bill at Babies"R"Us let us see and experience all of the new-fangled creations and apparatuses that would soon be part of our décor. We laughed at some of these items, researched some of them, and eventually bought some. But we were very selective. This world is competing for the love of our child, and we wanted her to be more in love with us than the material things we brought home. We wondered: *How do you balance the stuff and the opportunities that the world says your child needs with the words of God and His plan for your child?*

During my pregnancy, Psalm 139:13 became the verse that I latched onto, and this Psalm is still my favorite today. Why? Because it summarizes what I need to know about how much God loves and

knows me. As the passage continues, God reveals that He knew me
and fashioned me before I was born.

> For you **created** my inmost being;
> you knit me together in my mother's womb.
> I praise you because I am fearfully and wonderfully made;
> your works are wonderful,
> I know that full well.
> My frame was not hidden from you
> when I was made in the secret place,
> when I was woven together in the depths of the earth.
> Your eyes saw my unformed body;
> all the days ordained for me were written in your book
> before one of them came to be (Psalm 139:13–16 NIV).

In the first verse of this passage, the Hebrew word for "created" is
qana pronounced "kaw-naw."[2] The first time this word was used in the
Bible was when Eve gives birth to Cain (Genesis 4:1), but it is also used
throughout the Bible to describe God as Creator. The first time the
word is translated as "possessor" is in Genesis 14:19. In other verses,
the word is translated as "bought." Everything that God has created is
His. He is the "possessor" and the "purchaser" of everything created,
and everything includes our children. From the moment I read these
definitions, I knew that this child would not be ours. We were to be
the stewards and guardians to God's greatest creation, a child, who was
made in His image and fashioned with the physical merging of both
my husband's and my features and genes. The child would be pre-
programmed by God with a personality, and we would be helping him
or her understand what he or she was made to do so he or she could
fulfill God's calling for him or her. Some worldly philosophies imply
that we would be better off as cookie cutter humans, conformed to a
specific idea of perfection, success, and road to happiness, but those
of us who know and love our Creator know that each path is not the

same. As time went on, each time a decision came up that could affect Lilly's future, God would find a way to put Psalms 139 in front of me.

When you read the words in verse 14, "I am fearfully and wonderfully made" what comes to mind? For me, I wanted to know what God meant by "fearfully." With a little help from Strong's Concordance the Hebrew translation of the word *yare'* pronounced "yaw-ray," God gave me a revelation about how it was possible to feel as we raise our children. Two of Strong's definitions, in particular, stood out:

1. To cause astonishment and awe
2. To inspire reverence or godly fear or awe[3]

REALLY? So, we are to look at our children, no matter their age, with astonishment and awe. Watching them, we are to be inspired to give reverence to God for His creation using us as a vessel for His future arrows.

Continuing to break down the scripture, the next word I began to investigate was "wonderfully." Strong's again opens my eyes to how we would be wise to see our children. Our children should be...

1. distinct, marked out
2. separated, distinguished[4]

Every child has been created to be unique, separated from what the world would label them. When I looked in the *Oxford Learners Dictionary*, the root word "wonder" explained how I felt when I looked at our daughter.

A feeling of surprise mingled with admiration caused by something beautiful, unexpected, unfamiliar, or inexplicable.[5]

WOW! From this definition, it is clear to me that God is telling us to STOP looking at the world's definition of our children (physical, mental, and spiritual) and to START seeing their unique abilities. Those traits that tend to seem odd to everyone else are gifts given by God. In fact, in Psalm 139, David says, addressing God, "Wonderful are Your works" (Psalm 139:14b ESV). We would be wise, therefore, to watch our children for the wonderful gifts God has bestowed on them and to help them find ways to use those gifts. The next line of Psalm 139 says, "My soul knows it very well" (Psalm 139:14b ESV). Does your soul know your child well so that you as the warrior can help him or her use their gifts to hit God's target?

As we raise these little arrows, we need to ask ourselves daily if being afraid as parents is closing doors God wants to be open for our children. We are afraid our children will fail at school. We are afraid they will make a bad decision that could lead to an accident. We are afraid they will do something that will embarrass the family. Being afraid may cause us to hover too much, and therefore, we could stunt the growth they need to stay strong on the path of God's trajectory. We would be wise to remember that life has road bumps and to understand that we could get bruised along the way. It would also help us to remember that God could use each of these incidents or hurts for good in our children's futures.

Like a butterfly trying to escape the cocoon, the battle for freedom increases our children's strength so that they are prepared to face the calling God has for them. Being afraid as parents can delay the calling that Christ has for our children. Callings aren't just for adults; they actually start to develop at birth. And God had each child and his or her calling in mind long before each child was even conceived.

God was intentional when He used the word "arrow" to describe our children when His Word says: "Like arrows in the hands of a warrior are children born in one's youth" (Psalm 127:4 NIV). The process of preparing a reed or sapling to become an arrow is similar to that of a newborn baby. Once the saplings are cut, you tie them every few inches into tight bundles, to help them stay straight during the seasoning process. Seasoning is just a term to allow the wood to dry completely in a cool dry area for up to a year before the preparation of the arrow begins. Does this process remind you of anything?

Our "arrow reeds" are seasoning in the womb for nine months. And when they arrive, we clip the cord. Naked and cold, they are carefully placed on our chest. At the sound of a familiar heartbeat, the arrow relaxes, and a bond is re-created. Hearing familiar voices, these "arrows" stare up at us and try to share their language, so we as warrior parents can meet their every need. New cries reveal their needs from "I'm hungry!" to "I'm tired" to "Change me please!" We rush around trying to interpret each cry, while enjoying the quiet breaks with sweet smells and gentle coos when every need is met. As our "arrows" grow, they kick off the rest of the blanket, working all their limbs to prepare for the exploration of the world on their hands and knees.

Even though most of my friends told me about caring for the physical needs of my newborn baby, nobody really talked about wanting to sit and just watch the God-given internal learning ability develop. We looked at Lilly like a new piece of technology, whose workings were not quite understandable, and for which there was no manual. We were just as curious as she was about the new experiences that we were both sharing. Watching her made us seek God for direction. I believe God gave us this curiosity because He wanted us to watch carefully before we made decisions that could affect Lilly throughout her life. God wanted us to notice her for who He created her to be, not what we or the world thought she should become. I hear parents all the time say their babies are going to be ball players, musicians, or whatever else they imagine. Bill and I, however, had no big plans for Lilly. We just wanted to watch and see what God had for her—even if we didn't have a clue how to get her there.

Takeaway Transformation Tips for Parenting Our Arrows

- We would be wise, therefore, to watch our children for the wonderful gifts God has bestowed on them and help them find ways to use those gifts. #helpthemfindfaith
- Being afraid as parents can delay the calling that Christ has for our children. #beawarrior
- Callings aren't just for adults; they actually start to develop at birth. #helpthemfindfaith
- We were just as curious as she was about the new experiences that we were both sharing. Watching her made us seek God for direction. #beawarrior

Chapter Five

PROCURING SKILLS TO SHARE:
USING OUR UPBRINGING AND
EXPERIENCES

> For we are God's masterpiece. He has created us
> anew in Christ Jesus, so we can do the good things he
> planned for us long ago (Ephesians 2:10 NLT).

When you find out you are going to be a parent, I recommend sitting down for a substantial conversation with your spouse, during which each of you could share your experiences growing up to help steer your parenting journey. If you are already a parent, and you and your spouse are struggling, it's not too late to start to try to understand one another better. After you share, make a list of experiences you both want for your child so that you know you are both on the same page.

In this chapter, I'm including some of my husband's and my life's experiences, which we discussed that helped form our list for our daughter.

As I write, it has been forty-five years since my momma and daddy embarked on a journey owning and operating the ranch, which I shared about earlier. That journey affected my brother (my only sibling), myself, and my cousins in ways that will last for the rest of our lives. Momma is now eighty, and she says Daddy still wakes up in a cold sweat wondering what to do about the water/electricity and we are full to the brim with guests. Momma still cooks like she is cooking for fifty. Even today, when we all get together no matter how many years later, we can't help but remember a few stories of our adventures from our upbringing at Horseshoe Bend Guest Ranch. That is where God molded me, challenged me, and sometimes held me in the heart of the Rocky Mountains.

Like the words of John Denver in the song "Rocky Mountain High," I loved talking to God early in the mornings as I grew up on the ranch, and then waiting for His gentle whisper. That was my Rocky Mountain high.

I still long for the smell of fresh pine and the sound of the river's trickle, the crisp walk to the barn in the thirty-degree weather, which are all just a part of my DNA. Even today, when May rolls around, my husband says "my itch" acts up. I have to find some way to get outdoors, find the horses, and connect with my inner child.

My husband's childhood, which I also mentioned earlier, was completely different from mine. While I am the oldest, he is the youngest, and his siblings are much older. I never heard him call his parents Mom and Dad; he called them by their first names. He jokes that his parents told him to put up the matches when he finished playing with them. Both of his parents worked outside the home, and his family had a housekeeper who cared for him until he was old enough to go to school. His mom worked as a teacher, so he attended elementary school with her. As I mentioned, he spent summers away from his parents with his grandparents at the lake house, where he learned to drive a boat as a teen. From sixth through twelfth grade, he attended a private school while I went to a public school.

During my junior year in college, my parents decided to sell the ranch, and they moved to Florida. I finished college and lived near them. I traveled as a dancer and missionary, performing in theme parks and at dinner attractions. After an injury, I moved to another side of entertainment: working on films and editing videos.

Bill jumped into the film industry right out of college and had a great run as a video, film, and TV producer, as well as a sound engineer before he settled into IT (information technology). We met on a film set in our late twenties.

Fast forward several years…Bill and I were excited for the adventure of parenthood. Unlike Bill's mom, I wanted to be a stay-at-home mom, which meant he had to be confident that we could live on one income. Since Bill's family still owned the lake house, he looked forward to boat rides with our baby and eventually teaching him or her how to water ski, tube, drive the boat, and hike the nearby falls. He also couldn't wait to share stories about Mimi and Popi, the baby's great grandparents. Although he was excited to pass on his knowledge of life with our future child, he began to realize that being the youngest child, he never really held a baby, much less changed a diaper or fastened a car seat. Caring for a child would be a completely new experience for him.

My heart longed to give my child the same experiences I had growing up, but we did not have the means, especially with me wanting to be a stay-at-home mom. Nor did we have the desire to run a guest ranch. I asked myself: *What had I really learned through all those experiences that we could share without having the facilities?* We wanted our child to love the outdoors more than being inside. We wanted our child to experience boat rides with friends on lakes, hiking and camping in the forests, river rafting, and singing around a campfire with the guitar. We had both loved all these activities growing up. Before Bill and I got married, I also had an opportunity to deepen my love for horses and children working a summer job at a girls' camp…

The Camp Experiment

When I was about thirty, I had been praying for a new work situation. My particular video editing job required fast food because of short breaks, lots of caffeine because of long hours, and sitting on a chair in the dark in front of multiple television screens. Hearing about my upbringing outdoors, you can probably deduce that this environment wasn't my favorite. Add to that working for a boss who didn't share clear direction or empower me to make decisions…let's just say that it was really stressful.

The idea of becoming a teacher had been floating around in my head for a while during that season of my life, but I didn't want to go back to school, especially since part of me still wondered if teaching would be a good fit for me. I was resistant because college had been so tough for me; I had been diagnosed with dyslexia as a freshman. I knew it wouldn't be worth it to endure the difficulty of more education unless teaching was truly my calling.

To get into an environment that got me outside for at least a few hours a week while I continued to soul search, I took a weekend job as a horseback riding instructor. One Saturday morning, deprived from sleep after I had worked too late all week, I stumbled into the barn at 7 a.m., not knowing that this was the day that would lead me to beginning a new life. A friend I rode horses with that morning, Kelly, had been offered a job as the head of riding at a little girls summer camp in Vermont. She didn't want the job, so she introduced me to her friend Dottie, who also had connections at the camp. Dottie conducted a mini-interview with me and threw my name in the hat.

If I got the job, I would have an opportunity to teach the girls riding at summer camp. I would get to integrate what I was thinking about doing full time for a season without going back to school first. Dottie helped me get the job! Meeting her was a God moment and an answer to my prayers. I was so excited for a new adventure!

My parents have always been very supportive, but how do you announce that you're leaving your career for summer camp at the age of thirty? As I drove home, I rehearsed my speech over and over, until I had a plan, but once I was in the living room, it came out in usual Tammy fashion—I just said it. "Mom, Dad, I am quitting my professional job and going to work as the head of horseback riding at a summer camp in Vermont."

I was expecting a few questions of responsibility. I mean, after all, I owned a condo I had to pay for, I had a boyfriend of four years, and an established group of friends. But a litany of questions wasn't the response I got. My mom's eyes lit up, and you could see her wheels turning at Mach speed. My quiet-natured dad just shook his head with a big grin that left a twinkle in his eye. Immediately my mom said she would pack my trunk and told me she knew exactly what to pack. She had been a camper and then a counselor at the 4-H camp at Cherry Lake, Florida, for many years.

Dad asked to come with me on the twenty-two-hour drive from Jacksonville, Florida, to Fairlee, Vermont, in early June. That experience was such a joy. We reminisced about previous eighteen-hour trips we had made from Oklahoma to the ranch in Colorado and back again with horses and dogs every year for eight years. We drove up I-95 singing songs by John Denver and The Eagles, taking in the scenery as we crossed eleven state lines.

I so appreciated my parents' support of this decision—and them helping me in the transition. As Mom helped me get ready and Dad drove me, they exhibited the unconditional love that I would later try to model in my own parenting.

Once we arrived at the camp in Vermont, I took a deep breath. The smell of the pines brought me back to my childhood on the ranch. Dad and I walked through the pine-filled forest dotted with large army tents built on wooden platforms. We followed a dirt road that had two houses to our right on the hill. We passed another little shack like-home on the left as we continued to walk up the road to the back of the property. It was there that we found where I would begin my new career—in a small, run-down, wooden barn with a ring that was not much bigger than a tennis court. Some of the wooden boards from the barn had fallen onto the ground, and the weeds were growing in the crevices. I expected to see a tumbleweed roll by. The barn contained six standing stalls, about four by eight feet, with a couple of rings attached to the sides to clip the feed and water buckets to in each stall. Critters like mice, racoons, and pack rats had been hibernating in the barn during the winter, which I knew because of the holes in buckets, hay tucked neatly in corners, and droppings throughout the feed and tack room.

On the drive to take my dad back to the airport, he and I talked about what I envisioned for the camp. I told him I wouldn't be sure if the camp would be what I hoped for until I met the people I would be working for. As I pulled into the airport, a bit of sadness rumbled inside. I had forgotten how much I missed my trips with Dad. He got out of the car, and I gave him a big hug. He whispered in my ear, "This was a great decision." His affirmation meant the world to me in that moment, and it gave me an extra boost of courage as my new adventure began. This type of affirmation is something that Bill and I would later be intentional about passing on to our child.

I learned to shoot an arrow at camp—and archery became my favorite activity. The camp had a traditional bow with fiberglass arrows and the lines of release, which is the distance to the targets, were set at both ten and twenty feet. My first shot from ten feet included a nice welt on the inside of my left forearm. The injury happened from the bow string rubbing against my arm as I released the arrow. Keeping the bow string and the bow in alignment was more difficult than I thought. An eighteen-year-old camp counselor then gave me a few tips along with an arm guard to protect my new bruise. There was so much to learn, from the stance to pulling back the bow string to finding the right placement of the bowstring when you pull back the arrow near your cheek—all done while aiming directly at the center of the target. I dreamed of being Susan from Narnia on a horse aiming and shooting with precision as I rode through the mountains. As I learned archery, I had no idea that God would later help me apply archery lessons to parenting.

As I worked my first summer at the camp, I saw that God was giving me an education for the journey of a lifetime. He opened my eyes to see that He gives each of us the ability to learn, no matter our ages, if we take the opportunities He puts before us. Camp was the window where God showed me how He sees us as individuals and how He plants seeds of a calling in each one of us as well.

I learned not only the importance of my own choice that got me to the camp, but also I learned as the 149 female campers learned about choices and the effects of those decisions in their daily lives. They learned about their skills and interests as they chose activities, including basket weaving, archery, camping, lacrosse, or an array of water sports. The girls learned about compromise when they would choose morning activities to be with their friends, and they chose afternoon activities based on their interests. They became aware that they each had differing preferences and skills, and they began to understand that it was okay to be different from their friends.

The girls had fifteen activities to choose from ranging from arts and crafts, to drama, to hiking, sailing, and horseback riding. As the leaders of various activities, we advertised the entertainment for that day, and every camper had to choose how they would spend their time.

During the first week, I watched as campers would negotiate with friends where they were going for the first and second period, but as the time went on, the campers would find what they really liked, and they were able to forgo that time with a friend to focus on what made them happy.

Most of the campers came from life situations that didn't lend themselves to choices, whether they were wealthy from a penthouse on Fifth Avenue in New York City, or if they were there on scholarship from the poor side of Boston. Every turn had been decided for them. I learned about their lack of choices at home by interviewing the campers at meals, asking them if their choices at camp worked out for the day. I also asked them if they would have chosen differently if they could redo the day. During pre-camp, which is the time that the counselors prepare for the coming campers through building projects, planning agendas, and finding equipment, much of the training focused on choice. It wasn't until the campers arrived that I understood why; the campers needed to own their choices.

The campers weren't the only ones that learned while they were at camp. My obedience to follow God's path to summer camp taught me so much more than what I came to accomplish. He began to equip me with experiences I didn't know I needed. Not only did working at the camp confirm my direction for teaching, but the experience would also help me later as a parent. I learned how important it is to allow children to make some decisions early in life so that they are ready to make more significant choices later.

My obedience, including the choice I made to go work at the camp, made my life "go well," as it says in the following scripture.

> But I gave them this command: Obey me, and I will be your God and you will be my people. Walk in obedience to all I command you, that it may go well with you (Jeremiah 7:23 NIV).

For me, life going well meant that although I still made mistakes, I experienced peace, clarity, and joy in the midst of my journey. I received the peace and joy doing an activity I enjoyed in an environment where I loved working—being with the girls and horses, often outside. I gained clarity because the summer experience enabled me to have a taste of teaching, so I knew what God wanted me to do next—teach. Therefore, when I returned to Florida, my soon-to-be husband and I packed up and moved to Atlanta, where I had secured a teaching job. I started working as a computer teacher in an after-school program there. Eventually, the owner sold the company to me. I was able to hire more teachers and have an afterschool program in twenty more schools to educate elementary school students about how to use the computer for their schoolwork. Later, I began teaching various subjects in private schools and home school hybrids.

I was a full-time teacher for six years before I got pregnant. I knew that God would use both my experiences working at the camp and in teaching to help guide our child. These experiences also gave me information to share with Bill. We knew we needed to make some decisions about how discipline might work for us as parents so that we would be on the same page. Bill's parents had been laxer than mine because he was the third child. I, on the other hand, as the oldest, was not only responsible for myself, but sometimes my siblings as well. There were times I was punished right along with them even though I was not at fault. I didn't want a seemingly unjust approach for Lilly.

So, Bill and I agreed that her discipline would fall somewhere in the middle of strict and lax. Despite our different backgrounds, we were able to come together to understand one another and develop a plan. I'm going to put a pause on discipline here, but I'll come back to it in later chapters.

In addition to discipline, you will need to find common ground with your spouse on several other topics to steward your children as God's arrow. One of these topics is how to educate and care for your children at various times. I made the decision early on that I wanted to work from home, and because this is such an important topic in parenting, I want to give you a preview of how that decision turned out.

Once Lilly was old enough to be in school, I began teaching in each of the homeschool hybrid schools she attended. This decision added income, which allowed us to pay for her classes at these hybrids as well as to fund other extra-curricular activities, like sports, and experiences, such as going to museums or the theater. Teaching allowed me the flexibility to set my schedule so I could be available when our daughter needed me for extra help.

Like Bill and I, as a parent, you will need to make choices about caring for your child. In addition to caring for your child when you are with them, you will also need to discuss how childcare should be handled when you need help caring for them. Will you use babysitters, a nanny, or a care center? Finally, you will need to discuss how you will pursue medical care for a sick child or one with repetitive illness. Are you more of a Western medicine person, or do you and your spouse want to try alternative therapies at times? Having a plan for each of these topics in advance helped us lessen the conflict that so many spouses face.

As warriors, it is our job to prepare to shape our arrows as best we can. However, because we will not know the unique abilities our children have until they arrive, we will also need to learn to adapt in real time. No matter what your child's unique abilities may be, some of which the world will say are not normal, God chose you to be his or her warrior to mold an arrow, who will be part of a future generation. He also chose you to know these unique abilities and to find creative ways in which to help your arrow be shaped and eventually find flight.

Chapter Six

THE ARROW'S SHAFT: SEEING THE UNIQUE ABILITIES

For we are God's handiwork, created in Christ Jesus
to do good works, which God prepared in advance
for us to do (Ephesians 2:10 NIV).

Before arrow makers begin the process of creating the arrow, they look closely at each sapling (a young tree with a slender trunk) to see the individual wood's natural qualities. To make the best arrows, they need to understand the type of wood they are crafting before they begin the process of straightening. Knowing the type of wood will help the arrow maker correct the shaft without breaking it so it can fly straight. Most arrow makers use Port Orford Cedar, Sitka Spruce, and Douglas Fir for hunting arrows. These types of wood are not only strong but flexible. Many of our choices we made in parenting Lilly were to give her just that—strength and flexibility. I compare this process of learning about arrow making and understanding the wood choice of the warriors to watching other children in their early years before my baby came into the world.

I spent much of my time with other mothers while I was pregnant. I wanted to watch real life experiences and see the results. For exercise, I walked around my local park, and sat at the playground to rest. I not only interacted with my friends when I was with them, but also, I observed other mothers and children in the park. I regularly asked myself, *What was God showing me about differences in children and their gifts? What lessons did I want to take away for my future parenting?*

I would watch how various mothers dealt with tantrums. I would note whether they were conversational with their children or not, and I would watch how kids interacted with one another. I also babysat for friends in their homes. I noticed that some babies hum to the music at a very young age, sometimes less than six months old. As I made plans for my soon-to-be born child, I thought to myself, *I would buy a piano, but I wouldn't focus solely on the music. Instead, I would focus on teaching them the importance of using their gift to worship God.*

I also observed that by the time babies are crawling and a little more mobile, some begin to organize their toys in colors, sizes, or shapes. I made another mental note to myself that this innate organizational tendency could be important, as the babies might need or want that kind of order when it comes to learning. In the church nursery, I would see that some of the children had strong wills. I had heard this trait—being strong-willed—could be a sign of a future leadership gifting. My question as a future parent that developed out of that experience was, *How do you as the parent learn the skill to communicate with a growing lion?*

Throughout my pregnancy, I continued to work with children of all ages in schools and at camps, which continued to give me some insight into what I wanted and did not want to be as a mother. Most importantly, even though Bill and I had discussed it earlier as I mentioned, my experiences continued to affirm that I did not want to have a full-time job. Therefore, when I was pregnant, Bill and I decided that I would sell the afterschool computer business, keep the staff development classes, and create an advertising division for the public school system. These portions of the business would allow me to work part time from home and provide a little play money as we cut way back on our spending so we could live on one full-time income. I had seen so many of my friends struggling to continue to live the lavish lifestyle, which required them to return to work only six weeks after birth. Their hearts were crushed as they left their new babies at the daycare.

Here She Comes

> May he give you the desire of your heart and make all
> your plans succeed (Psalm 20:4 NIV).

Having our one and only child at age thirty-six gave me plenty of time
to think about how I would apply the knowledge I had amassed from
teaching to child rearing as well as many opportunities to pray about
what God wanted for this new precious gift. So, when I was pregnant,
we simply dedicated our child to God and we focused on praying for
our child to be all that God would want him or her to be, and for us
to remember we are only the steward of this little arrow. We knew that
someday he or she would fly off on his or her own, so our job was to
prepare our child for battle. Like arrows in the hands of a warrior, as I
have mentioned, we as parents are the senior warriors training our
young warriors for their future battles in their adult lives. We had
always heard that eighteen years went by faster than we could possibly
imagine, and there were so many things we wanted to share with her—
we were going to need Him to direct our steps!

We also knew, as I have mentioned, that there is a war for our kids'
lives being waged from the minute of conception. Pregnancy is not a
time to let your guard down; it is a time to start facing the battles ahead
on your knees. I was on my knees often, but during my eighth month,
I needed Bill's help to get up afterwards! I was so excited for the grand
reveal and the arrival of our arrow that God had to remind me that
everything would happen in His timing—not before.

Lilly had a hard entrance into the world. After twenty plus hours
of labor, I was wheeled into the operating room for a C-section. She
was beautiful, with a head full of dark brown hair that nurses swooned
over as they visited me in the recovery room. While I was in my little
mommy moment, breathing in deep the scent of this wonderful gift,
some of the family began to wonder about her special little hand. As I
have shared, Lilly has a banded right hand that consists of just a palm

and a half of a thumb, but I didn't care. I knew she was perfect in God's eyes, and I also knew that He had a plan beyond all of our plans.

For a few months, people would ask what Bill and I were going to do about her hand. After much prayer for God to show us what He wanted us to do, the answer came in the checkout line at Target. As I waited for the gentleman in front of me to check out, I played peek-a-boo with Lilly. She was always a happy girl, and we giggled until something caught my eye. The gentleman pulled out a twenty-dollar bill to pay. I looked over to the young man working the register, who was about seventeen, as he began to pull change. His right hand was just a thumb and forefinger, while his left arm looked as if it had been amputated at the mid forearm. When the register opened, he placed the twenty-dollar bill to the right side of the register and put his left arm against the drawer. He pulled out a five and three ones with his right fingers, he laid the money on his left arm along the drawer making a shallow dip, and then counted the change onto the bills. He shut the drawer with his hip as he used his right hand to balance the change and give it to the man. I took a deep breath and gave a moment of praise to my Father—I knew He had provided an answer.

He began to ring up my cart when I said, "Excuse me, I know this is a very personal question, and you don't have to answer if you don't want to, but what do I do with this?" I held up Lilly's hand, and he began to laugh. "No bother, just let her figure it out. My parents have this box in the back of the garage, which is where they store the stuff they bought or created to help me eat and write. They tried to bend silverware and to make pipe cleaner holders for my pencils to help me hold them. But in the end, I just figured out how to use real silverware and how to write with a regular pencil. Those interesting creations are still in the box in the garage. She will be fine."

I smiled gratefully as he handed me my receipt. As we left, I began to tear up because I knew that was the Holy Spirit speaking through this young man, and his words were all I needed to hear.

I told my husband what had happened, and we agreed to let her figure everything out, from eating to writing, to climbing the monkey bars and riding a bike. This would be her journey, not ours. We were sent by God to think outside the box and to be the support and prayer team along the way. This philosophy of stepping back and being the silent partner as she figured things out is how Lilly was raised differently than some. She was never told she couldn't do something because of her disability, and that mindset translated across all aspects of her life. Her doing anything meant us stepping back, giving her space to learn what she could do—and what she couldn't do—without us intervening. She needed to know her limitations, and she needed to know when to ask for help. She also learned to jump for joy at every triumph. From the beginning, this was HER journey.

Seeing Her Unique Abilities

We chose to see Lilly's disability through God's eyes, as a "unique ability." We told her that God made her special, which is why she has a little hand and a big hand too. Thanks to the movie *Finding Nemo*, we also referred to her hand as her little fin. Nemo never let his little fin keep him from exploring his world and participating in it. He was a great example of someone who stepped up to the challenge with his unique ability. Looking past her diagnosis of a banded hand helped us see how God's unique vision for our child would one day fulfill His calling for her.

When children have unique abilities, many of us tend to seek help from medical professionals for solutions. But how many of us seek answers outside the world's norm and look past a label or diagnosis to see how that child's unique abilities could be applied to life? Unique abilities come in many forms: physical, mental, or learning challenges. Children with unique abilities all need an out-of-the-box approach when they are being reared. It helped us to remember that our child is OUR gift from God. She was not created by the doctors and other professionals, nor was she their gift to steward. God created your children perfectly in His eyes, and He gave them this uniqueness because He is inviting them to fulfill His plan.

CHILDREN ARE LIKE ARROWS IN THE HANDS OF A WARRIOR

We have no idea what our children's futures hold, so we as Christians need to seek God's Word for direction in which to channel our child's uniqueness. I am not saying we forgo the medical community and their diagnoses; I am saying we need to seek God before choosing the medical solutions over what God might be calling us to lay aside to help us learn more about our child. Listen to the Holy Spirit when something doesn't sit well with you in therapy, with meds, or with educational choices. Question those in charge and seek alternatives.

My brother and I talk regularly about how he would have been diagnosed with ADHD and put on meds if he was born today. But our mom, with a degree in nutrition and child psychology, chose a solution that included diet—not meds—lots of soccer, and being prepared with her big bag of tricks. Then she held on to every little success, even though it felt like some of them came with three steps backwards. Todd wasn't necessarily a bad kid, but sometimes curiosity would get the best of him. Mom figured out he just needed to play hard so he could focus. In high school, Todd played on three soccer teams. On weekends, my dad taught him how to rebuild anything, including cars and electronics, and now he is a master craftsman in construction. The time my parents spent with Todd taught him that there are times when concentration is important. They also helped him find what activities would help him concentrate, and for him, those were things that involved being outside.

When our children have unique abilities, we also see them suffer. Many times, as parents, we suffer with our kids. Teaching your child to walk away when someone is hurtful is hard, but we need to teach them to turn the other cheek and pray for those who persecute them. Unfortunately, when we feel their hurt and their pain, we tend to deal with the problem ourselves rather than have our child participate in the solution. This makes it your solution, not THEIR solution, and if we handle the situation this way, we have taught them that Mommy and Daddy will fix the problem. If you want to fix your child's problem yourself, stop, get on your knees, and pray. Ask the Holy Spirit to help you help your child find solutions, and then help your child put those answers into action. This type of problem solving is a skill that will follow them into adulthood. Without you helping them to develop this independent mindset, they might be living in your basement until they are thirty.

Although it's not good to do everything for your child, it is helpful to look for adults with your child's unique ability to share their insights with both you and your child. Just be open and ask God to show you. He is faithful! He may use someone unexpected just like He did when He gave me His answer through the mouth of a seventeen-year-old store clerk. We also prayed for God to provide someone older who has a similar hand as Lilly's. We prayed that person would tell Lilly stories and challenge her to continue to break through any limitations to activities she might want to accomplish. And God heard us. A family friend introduced us to a gentleman about our age whose hand was indeed like Lilly's. This connection provided a great opportunity for Lilly to ask him questions that we could not answer. After he spoke to Lilly for the first time, he came to me and said, "WOW! She is doing so much better than I was at eight. Her faith is strong, and you can see that she understands that this is a uniqueness not an "imperfection.""

Just like when Lilly's faith encouraged this man when we were seeking help, God will use children and people who the world sees with a limitation in ways we can't predict to bless others. I have heard story after story about how God used a terminally-ill child to reach the hearts of doctors, nurses, and others because they show a joy in Christ that can't help but be noticed. I smile when I think of the contagious happiness of Down syndrome adults who share their enthusiasm with the world as they carry our groceries. Sometimes we need to step back and see what God sees, so that we can let our little ones show us how circumstances should be handled in response to those unique abilities. Multiple times God "WOWED" us.

A friend of mine from high school had a brain tumor, and people would stare and pull their children away from him. He loved telling kids why he was bald and had a tube on his head. Kids are naturally curious, so don't be that freaked out parent when your child wants to ask a question of someone who looks different or has a disability. Let them ask. Their curiosity gives them an understanding that will build their compassion for those who are different from themselves.

At the age of fifty-nine, I look back and see how often we, as parents, unintentionally hinder our children by limiting their abilities because we do not think they are old enough, strong enough, or brave enough to do what God might be calling them to do at age three, ten, or fifteen. I say three because I once saw a three-year-old kid lead another kid to Jesus at the park. Witnessing that experience taught me that God has a calling on all our lives from the minute we are born, not when we turn thirteen, sixteen, or twenty-five. From the moment our children enter our families, God wants us to remember that they are only with us for a short time. During their time with us, we are commanded to teach them the truth of the Bible, and to be an example of service to others. We are to show them that God is our provider, to encourage their relationships with Him, and to help them seek His calling. Once again, I will say: we are told to, "Train up a child in the way he should GO; even when he is old he will not depart from it" (Proverbs 22:6 ESV, capital letters added for emphasis).

Kingdom Thinking

Cleaning and straightening a shaft of an arrow is not a quick process. First, you must prepare a sharp object such as a sharp stone. With your sharp object, you begin to strip the bark piece by piece, and like opening a gift God created, you watch as the beauty is revealed. The bark can be beautiful in color, but it is only there for the protection of the branch. Once the branch is cut, the bark no longer protects the branch from death or damage, but in the right hands, the branch will be repurposed.

Like the bark of the shaft, the womb protects the baby, and the beauty of the woman carrying the child is something to behold. When the baby is born, the birth could be compared to starting the removal of bark from the tree. That baby is then in the hands of the parent as he or she is being prepared for a purpose. The sharp object that we as parents continue to use for this debarking process is the sword of the Spirit, known as the Word of God.

The world wants you to think that success is money, wealth, and freedom to say and do what you please, but according to the Word of God, success in the kingdom comes from immediate obedience to the Father. In this book, I refer to this principle as "kingdom thinking." Paul speaks many times about his suffering because obedience to a call for Christ may include suffering. Although sometimes a person may be considered successful in their godly calling by worldly standards, it is possible that a godly calling may not include worldly success. We have to show our children that in their suffering, God always provides something for which to be thankful. In Philippians, Paul explains in simple words what kingdom thinking is:

> Rejoice in the Lord always. I will say it again: Rejoice!
>
> Let your graciousness be known to everyone. The Lord is near.
>
> Don't worry about anything, but in everything, through prayer and petition with thanksgiving, present your requests to God.
>
> And the peace of God, which surpasses all understanding, will guard your hearts and minds in Christ Jesus.
>
> Finally brothers and sisters, whatever is true, whatever is honorable, whatever is just, whatever is pure, whatever is lovely, whatever is commendable—if there is any moral excellence and if there is anything praiseworthy—dwell on these things.
>
> Do what you have learned and received and heard from me, and seen in me, and the God of peace will be with you (Philippians 4:4–9 CSB).

From the beginning of these verses, we see that the most important part of kingdom thinking is thankfulness. When you are grateful for every aspect of your life, knowing that your journey will be used by God in the future, you know that any hardships will be worth it. With that thankfulness, Jesus promises peace that will protect our heart and mind, if we allow it to. You may ask, *How does that peace happen in the midst of difficulty?* In verse 8 of the passage we just read, Paul is telling us how. We focus on what is true, honorable, just, pure, lovely, commendable, and of moral excellence. Try to find these attributes in every circumstance, and you will see a God thread or lesson emerge from even difficult situations. In my journey, I wish I would have fully adopted the attributes in the verse I just mentioned and seen a God thread sooner.

As a schoolteacher and a homeschool mom, many people have asked me questions about several issues such as instilling confidence in children, determining the best age to give children chores, or teaching children responsibility so that they get out of bed for school, clean their room, and develop good hygiene. I am sympathetic! We were those parents lost in the crossroads of child rearing in a sea of information.

When I was pregnant or as I was raising Lilly, many friends gifted me books or gave me book recommendations. Countless comments were given from friends, family, and doctors who all meant well, but none of these books or ideas pointed us to Jesus and His Word. Because I was a believer, I wanted God's input more than worldly knowledge, but none of the information I found focused on biblical principles. The following questions kept playing like an echo on a carousel in my head: *Do we follow what the world says we need to do for a child to have success? Do we sit back and let the child make all the rules?* (We saw children making the rules in so many families, we began to think this was a new parenting style.) *Why isn't the church more specific about teaching us how to raise children with God as their targets?* Over time, not seeing the answers I wanted to these questions as well as having so many people ask me questions through the years caused me to want to write this book!

Takeaway Transformation Tips for Parenting Our Arrows

- The world wants you to think that success is money, wealth, and freedom to say and do what you please, but according to the Word of God, success in the kingdom comes from immediate obedience to the Father. #helpthemfindfaith

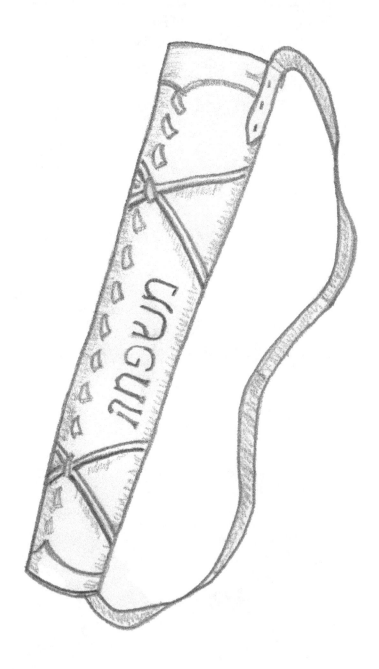

Chapter Seven

YOUR QUIVER: DOING LIFE WITH YOUR FAMILY IN TOW

All your children will have GOD for their teacher—
what a mentor for your children! (Isaiah 54:13 MSG).

"Make this baby adaptable" was my husband's constant prayer during my pregnancy. We were very active people, and we were both very excited about this new bundle. But in some ways, I think we were worried about not being able to get up and go. Bill's parents were a whole generation older than mine, and when we were talking about starting a family, my husband actually said, "I don't want to be as old as my dad when I have a kid." It was just then that he realized he was only a year away from thirty-eight, the age of his dad when he was born. We were busy people. As I mentioned, I owned an afterschool computer education business for kindergarteners through fifth graders, and I also taught continuing education courses for teachers, which they need for required staff development credit. We also traveled to officiate mountain bike races, and we loved serving in our church. My parents, unlike Bill's, were in their early twenties when I was born, and as kids, we did whatever they did. And that is how my husband and I, along with our village, raised our daughter.

As new parents, we tend to hang on every word of those who seem more experienced than us. We combed through the parenting magazines to find new techniques to help the baby sleep, we looked for advice about when and what to feed them, and we wanted recommendations about what brand of disposable diaper is best for the baby's skin. But I wondered what happened to the old tried and true, long time, traditional parenting techniques—techniques that worked when our great grandparents parented strong, independent, self-reliant children into adults. I wanted to engage in parenting that included participation in family "chores"—washing the dishes, hanging the clothes on the line, and feeding the animals because participating in what had to be done was how I was raised. Some would say I turned out a little eccentric, but they would also say I was more confident and adventurous. How do we instill that confidence and spirit of adventure in our children?

When I was pregnant, my mom mentioned an old wives' tale about how to put the baby to sleep by rubbing my belly and singing a song over my womb when I went to sleep. Then as I awoke, I would wake her up in my womb by bouncing my belly. This method was supposed to put our babies on a set schedule. IT WORKED! Lilly slept through the night right out of the womb, for almost seven hours. That first night in the hospital, I got a little nervous when it occurred to me that Lilly had not woken up for her feeding. I had read that just after birth, it should be no more than four hours between feedings. So, I rang the nurse who quickly told me "You never wake a sleeping baby."

From the moment Lilly joined our family, we took her everywhere, like an arrow in a quiver. Lilly was always with us, literally going from the womb to a Dr. Sears Sling Carrier, which was made of cute denim plaid with padded siding. During my pregnancy, I read about "wearing your child." I learned that the reason for doing this in tribal history was for safety, but more recent studies showed that children tend to have less separation anxiety if they are worn. My friend bought the sling for me when I sent her on an errand. The sling was comfortable for both Lilly and me. It provided so much coverage that I could teach my adult classes, and she could nurse without anyone knowing, until she slurped. It fit across my chest like a sash for a queen. I wore her like an accessory to every outfit, or did she wear me? She hung on either Bill or me to the point where she would only sleep if her body was swinging in the sling. I learned to move her to the nursing pillow to rest her little bum in the hole while she was still in the sling, so she could sleep without me. When she awoke, I slipped her back on, and off we went. When Bill would come home from work, we would transfer the sling from my body to his, with Lilly inside. It was like moving a cargo container from the boat to the semi. If we were out and about, I wore the sling, and she could be found in it. When she would hear a voice that was new to the conversation, you would see her little arm swing out of the cocoon, and her little face turn to see who it was. If she wanted to be a part of the conversation, she would peek out. If not, back into the dark she would go.

From festivals and events to movies and campaigns to church programs, Lilly was with us. Lilly traveled around as a passenger in a backpack on a hike to the falls. She hung in the sling when we attended the Steeple Chase. She came with us when we went fox hunting. When I say she went everywhere, I mean everywhere. There were always people we knew on these adventures, so she got to know everyone as she toddled around checking out whatever was going on.

We had seen many babies in car seats at events and in strollers, but we eventually learned that what we read about using the Dr. Sears slings was true—they helped lessen separation anxiety at the toddler phase. We saw that as Lilly grew into a toddler, she had little to no separation anxiety. Other people noticed too! We knew that her being in the sling gave her a confidence that allowed her to experience her little world without the fear of feeling like we were going to leave her. The National Institute for Health has recognized that there are benefits of baby wearing to both baby and parent. Being hands free the parent can do other tasks while the baby feels comforted by the presence of the parent. Oxytocin, the love hormone, is also released when a baby is worn, allowing positive effects on mood and bonding.[6] Before Lilly walked, we only put her in the car seat when we would eat or to travel.

Speaking of food, we knew we were not going to feed her the usual baby food. When Lilly was four months old, my breast milk began to dry up, so we needed to switch to formula. We never heated a bottle, we just poured room temp water into the bottle with the formula and gave it a shake. My understanding with friends is that once you heat a bottle that baby will always want a heated bottle. We were just too mobile for that. Once she could eat solid food, we bought a blender, and she ate what we ate. I would always make some extra veggies and then blend them and put them in ice trays in the freezer. That way, when we went out to eat, or she couldn't eat our food, I could just pull out the food trays, pick a few squares, and put them in a plastic zipper top baggy. By the time our food came to the table at a restaurant, her food would be thawed and ready to eat.

The diaper dilemma was a big thing for me. We saw right away that Lilly was allergic to every disposable diaper we tried on her. Early in my pregnancy, I had decided that I wanted cloth diapers. I just couldn't figure out how to get past the mess and smell. Fortunately, my sister-in-law had a solution. She gave us a month's subscription to Diaper Dans! Love them! Diaper services have so much to offer the mom and the baby, not to mention the environment. We did the numbers, and the price was comparable to the cost of disposables. When you look for a service (they are few and far between), they should provide you with a choice of how many diapers, a hamper with a deodorizer, and a selection of with or without scented cleaners. Also, you don't want to pre-rinse the diapers before you put them in the hamper. When the hamper is full, just tie up the bag and place it outside for pick-up and delivery. I had been to many friends' homes who had the Diaper Genie for their disposable diapers, and I could always smell the dirty diapers. When friends would come to my house, they were shocked that there was no odor. Forget the clothes pins to hold the diaper on! You can get cute diaper wraps that Velcro—all in various sizes and colors. And for wipes, I would use cheap washcloths from Walmart that I would cut into four pieces. I would then dampen the cloths before I put them in a zipper top baggy. I would carry an extra plastic baggie to put the used wash rag squares in, and then I would throw them in the washer when I got home.

Everyday there were places to go, especially church, where Bill and I were involved in many ministries. Lilly was fine to be on Bill's lap on a Thursday night as he did sound for rehearsal while I sang. She could also be with me at a kid-sale fundraiser in her backpack carrier as I helped organize clothing. Starting at around age three or four, we gave her a job at every turn. At the kid sale, a used clothing and toy sale for raising church funds, she handed me hangers and sorted things by color. She was my enthusiastic worshipper at band practice, and she helped me cook at home. She was my little helper.

As she got older, she worked with us as we packed meals for the hungry, sorted clothing for a consignment sale, and prepared food for sick people, various events, and parties. She lived life with us, and through those experiences, she learned skills she could use in the future to serve her community.

So many parents I talk with live a separate life from their kids, by choice. In the kitchen, they prepare the kids' lunches for school, and they don't want help. Every day, we as parents tend to complain about how tired and overwhelmed we are. Yet God has prepared helpers for us in our children. Yes, it will take longer to make the lunches if your children participate, but what if you made the meals after dinner, and you showed them the acceptable foods that go into the next day's lunch? What if you showed them how to make a sandwich or how to ladle leftover soup into a thermos? Before too long, they will be able to do these tasks themselves, and all you have to do is inspect their work. Not to mention that you just gave them a little taste of independence.

The best way to figure out when children are old enough to do a particular activity is to have him or her by your side mimicking you. Doing laundry, preparing a meal, organizing the receipts and typing them in Quicken, taking out the trash, cleaning the bathrooms, vacuuming—the list your children can learn to do is endless. All of these tasks can be done by your helpers if you take the time to show them how you want these things done. To start, give your children a small part of whatever task you are doing, like separating the colors of laundry. You will need to talk them through the process as you do it. Talking out loud will not only help your child, but also it may help you

CHILDREN ARE LIKE ARROWS IN THE HANDS OF A WARRIOR

stay focused on what you are doing too. As I write this book now that Lilly is grown and out of the house, I find that I still talk to myself as I do various processes as a habit. It also won't be too long before I have grands following me around, and then I'll use this process whenever I care for them, too.

I think we forget that having chores fosters self-discipline and that helping each other strengthens our bonds. Help your children understand how they can love by teaching them the following verse from 1 John, which says, "Dear children, let us not love with words or speech but with actions and in truth" (1 John 3:18 NIV). *Did you catch that?* We love each other "with actions and in truth," This verse reminds me of a book, *The Five Love Languages,* by Gary Chapman. Dr. Chapman offers a test to help you discover the love languages of each of your family members. To take the test, go to the Resources page at the end of this book, where I've added a link. A person's love languages sometimes change as we age, so redo the test every few years. Put a copy of everyone's love language on the front of the fridge. This note helps everyone know how to love one another. Many times, we don't share the same love language as other members of the family. I've said this many times, but it's worth repeating: *You have to be intentional about when and how you love each other.* The other fun activity is teaching your kids to love even if they don't receive recognition. This understanding creates a willingness in them to do right when no one is looking. In other words, you are helping them build their character.

Carrying your quiver full of arrows can be heavy at times, so make sure both parents carry the load from time to time. I know traditionally it has been the mom who stays at home with the children and does the house responsibilities, but nothing in the Bible says the person who stays home has to be the mom. The father can be the stay-at-home dad and do it just as well. If both of you can work from home, that can be a benefit, but only if you set some ground rules for yourselves to ensure that you stick to those rules. I love that in my own childhood, because of our family's business, I learned how parents can work together and help their children find a purpose at a young age by helping their parents side by side. Remember, after God and your spouse, your main focus in this world is the greatest gift God can give—stewarding your children. So, make every day count as you live life with your children.

Takeaway Transformation Tips for Parenting Our Arrows

- From the moment your child joins your family, take them everywhere, like an arrow in a quiver. #beawarrior

Chapter Eight

→→→————————————→

CHOICE...WITH CONSEQUENCES

The LORD God placed the man in the Garden of
Eden to tend and watch over it. But the LORD God
warned him, "You may freely eat the fruit of every
tree in the garden—except the tree of the knowledge
of good and evil. If you eat its fruit, you are sure to
die" (Genesis 2:15–17 NLT).

Since the creation of man, God has gifted us with choices. God gave
Adam plenty of fragrant fruit trees to choose from. The consequences
of eating fruit from any of these trees would have been one of
enjoyment and life. God had warned Adam to not eat from the tree of
the knowledge of good and evil. God's warning of death meant little
to Adam; he was not aware of what death was. And yet, Adam was still
given the choice to eat the forbidden fruit. Satan's twisting of words
when he spoke to Eve were not the same as the words spoken by God
to Adam. Her choice to eat came through deception, yet she still chose
to disobey, and the consequences were immediate.

There was no hesitation in God's punishment. In Genesis, we read
"But the LORD God called to the man, 'Where are you?'" (Genesis 3:9
NIV). God knew what had happened, but notice God calls to Adam
first. God gave the command to Adam. Eve wasn't even present; she
heard it second hand. Giving Adam a chance to own up to his
disobedience, God asks him, "Who told you that you were naked?
Have you eaten from the tree that I commanded you not to eat from?"
(Genesis 3:11 NIV). Immediately, Adam tried to distance himself from
the sin by playing the blame game. But God didn't hesitate to give the

punishment. He quickly responded, explaining the reason for the punishment and what it was going to be.

> To Adam he said, "Because you listened to your wife and ate fruit from the tree about which I commanded you, 'You must not eat from it,'
> "Cursed is the ground because of you;
> through painful toil you will eat food from it
> all the days of your life.
> It will produce thorns and thistles for you,
> and you will eat the plants of the field.
> By the sweat of your brow
> you will eat your food
> until you return to the ground,
> since from it you were taken;
> for dust you are
> and to dust you will return."
> Genesis 3:17–19 (NIV)

Just as God's discipline to Adam's disobedience was immediate, our response to our disobedient children needs to be straightforward and quick. Delay stirs up strife and begins to build a wall in communication from both sides. Another lesson we learn from the preceding passage is that the consequences for Adam and Eve's actions are specific and different for the man and the woman. These distinct consequences show us that God sees a difference in each of us, and He knows our understanding of our punishments will be different. Every consequence, both bad and good, should include a full explanation of what the response is and why that response is appropriate. These responses need to be specific to each child, just as they were for Adam and Eve.

As adults, we make hundreds of choices each day that affect not only us but also our families. Where did we learn this skill of choice? How did we get good at making the right choices? Was it through trial and error? How old were we when we started making choices? We began giving our daughter choices as soon as she could point.

When is the Best Time for Children to Start Choosing?

My husband and I believe that children need to start making choices that affect them as soon as they start pointing. I am not saying they should make ALL CHOICES, but there are choices a child can make that fit different ages. When Lilly was playing with toys as a baby, we would always give her two toy choices before we put her into the crib for a nap. She was the first grandchild, and she received an abundance of gifts that were overwhelming for us and for her. We chose to limit how many things were available to play with in her room at any one time. Three, maybe four, larger toys would be available, with eight to ten smaller ones including education and imagination toys, like mega blocks and puzzles. We didn't limit the number of books she had because we wanted her to enjoy reading.

About once a month, we would take one of the larger toys she no longer showed interest in, and we would swap it out and prep the old, large toy for sale at a kid sale or consignment store. We did the same with smaller toys. This practice helped lessen clutter, and Lilly was excited when we put a new toy in her room. Most of the time, she never noticed the old toy was gone.

To allow Lilly to do life with me as I did daily household chores, there were certain staple toys—or should we say stable toys—throughout our house. Lilly loved horses because she had played at the barn with her best friend, Casey, while I gave riding lessons part time at a stable. Since I loved horses as well, I placed a rocking horse in every room of our home. This way, she could both play with the horses and be with me as I did the housework, dishes, and laundry. My husband and I wanted to foster her imagination, and God just laid the idea in my head about mimicking the set-up of the stable in our home. Just like at any barn, the toy horses had different names and colors. I would converse with her about the adventure she was on while she was riding Blaze or Bullet, which were names she got from television shows or books. We still laugh about how at one point my husband remarked that the "stable" in our home was full—and I wasn't "allowed" to bring anymore rocking horses home!

Also, when Lilly was two, I decided she was old enough to pick out her clothes. As parents, we know those clothes are coming off if our children don't like them. So, I was thinking that I wouldn't have to dress Lilly over and over again throughout the day if she picked out her clothes herself. The frustration Lilly showed when trying to dress herself without fingers gave us the chance to teach her about self-control. We taught her how to take a deep breath and refocus. Every time she would get frustrated, one of us would say, "Deep breath," and eventually as she grew, it became her go to saying—even when we aren't around. Even today as an adult, I see Lilly take a deep breath before she attempts something challenging to her hand. But when she was two, the look on her face when she figured out how to pull on pants without my help was priceless. Turning her shirt right side out was also unforgettable. But the flip side of Lilly picking out her clothing was that she usually left the house in a tutu, t-shirt, pink cowboy boots, and a cowboy hat. I would just smile and put her in the car. At least she wore a clean t-shirt every day.

This pattern repeated because every morning we would talk about what we had planned for the day, and she would go into her room and get dressed. As I've mentioned, when she was only two, we laid some ground rules that we hoped would carry her from childhood into adulthood. We separated the closet into play clothes, going out clothes, church clothes, and costumes. This practice helped her know that when we say the word "church," that these are the clothes we would prefer she pick out. She could still choose to wear other clothing, but since it was one day a week, dressing like a princess made her feel special.

Challenge Through Choice

Teaching children about choice requires us as parents to put choices in front of them every day. Sometimes our children's choices have good consequences. For example, if they choose a coat that is made for the weather, and they are about to walk into rain or snow, they will not get wet. Sometimes the choices have bad consequences, like if they pretend to be a cop running into a door to break it down like in the movies, which will likely result in an injury. Children don't understand that the stunt man in the movies runs through a hollow door. Sometimes children have to learn the consequences of their choices through the school of hard knocks, but they can practice choices like they would any other skill if we as parents allow the consequences to happen to them.

If your child is afraid of heights, start by helping them overcome being afraid by giving them a choice of things to climb. You can vary the heights depending on where your child is at, but the goal is to get him or her to see that climbing is not scary. Most kids love to climb if they don't equate climbing to the top of the slide with being afraid of heights. Instead, they are focused on the fun of sliding. If you as the parent put your children at the top of slides yourself, you have denied them the challenge of choosing to climb. Sometimes children need the chance to look at scary things from the perspective of other kids doing those scary things. Other times a little encouragement from you is just the push they need to try something new. Be patient and give them time to watch and participate at their own pace, then cheer them on. Don't make a big deal out of the situation if they fail. Ask them how they could accomplish the task a different way and then help them see the alternatives and encourage them to try again. Keep giving them experiences that will challenge their bodies, minds, and souls.

The playground is a great place to challenge kids physically. Puzzles will challenge their minds. And stories with heroic endings will give them the desire to want to be heroes in the future, challenging their souls. Keep the choices coming when they are small, so that they are ready to participate in the bigger ones...like school.

Picking a School

One way we allowed Lilly to have choices was to have her involved in decisions about her education. Deciding when and where to send your child to any type of childcare/preschool is always a challenge. We knew that we would not be taking the traditional route of public school. As I mentioned, I had been a county schoolteacher, and I had seen the lack of focus on the basics. I also saw teachers being reprimanded for teaching to the students' individual needs rather than the set curriculum, which I also feel is not in the best interest of students. These challenges in public schools sent us looking for another type of school for Lilly. We wanted more of a classical foundation, so we chose to homeschool. At two, we began taking Lilly to a Mom's Day Out program two days a week at our local recreational center. Being a little socialite, she loved getting to spend time with friends her own age and learn new things. She enjoyed being a part of that program, and we wanted her to continue into that organization's pre-K program. But when the time came for registration, we ran into a snag because this pre-K program didn't allow students who knew how to read. Lilly had taught herself to read when she was three. I know that sounds odd, but it really happened.

We had read with Lilly every night, and sometimes also before nap time. Every child has their favorite books, and Lilly began to say all the words with us. One day she came into the kitchen and read me a story. It was one of our favorites, so I congratulated her on her accomplishment and moved on. I assumed she had memorized the book and was reading from memory. She would have none of the, "It's time to move on" signals I was giving her. So, she went and found a book that we had read maybe a couple times and sat down. She figured out how to pronounce eighty percent of the words on her own. Since Lilly could read and the pre-K wouldn't allow that, we found a homeschool hybrid, RCA. A staff member there interviewed Lilly and said she was ready for kindergarten.

She might have been ready, but I was not. Being a teacher, I watched kids struggle when they started school too young, and I wanted Lilly to be a champion at school. My husband graduated at seventeen, and he too was nervous, but we basically told God that if she gets accepted, we would follow that path. Lilly said she wanted to go to RCA, so we signed her up.

Each year as school would finish, we would have a conversation with her about where she wanted to attend school the following year. We wanted Lilly to have input.

I'd say, "Lilly, where do you want to go to school next year? We have to plan now so we can let the school know."

"Could I ride the big yellow bus?" she asked.

"If you go to Mountain Park Elementary, you can ride the big yellow bus," I replied.

"Do they go to school on Fridays?"

"Yes, every Friday."

"Okay, I want to stay at RCA."

It was clear that she didn't want to go to school on Fridays! Years later, with a laugh, I can look back and see that her choice remained consistent. Throughout Lilly's education, she never attended school on Friday, even when she was in college.

How did we continue to foster that decision-making resolve? We kept her involved in her learning process. Providing an atmosphere of learning at home can really plant a foundation of curiosity that will keep your children moving forward in their education. Before I give you more ideas of how we did that in our home, let me tell you what NOT to do—because it's just that important! DO NOT rely on video games and unsupervised time in front of the television to teach your toddler through elementary aged children. Screen time removes the desire for interpersonal communication skills, impedes patience, and lessens the tolerance necessary for effective learning. We did not allow Lilly to have any technology or video games until she was about age ten. Babies need physical stimulus and human communication that shows them how to relate to other humans. They need to touch and feel, and to hold and manipulate physical items.

CHILDREN ARE LIKE ARROWS IN THE HANDS OF A WARRIOR

Studies have now shown that the technology age has changed our children's neurological processing and those who teach have seen the change. Dr. Dimitri Christakis is the leading author of the American Academy of Pediatrics' guidelines for screentime. He explains that screen addiction has bigger implications to infants than adolescents. The press of a button is building an artificial stimulation of instant gratification through a dopamine rush. It isn't that they can't do virtual tasks; the fact is that they shouldn't do them. His studies show that the brain development of an 18–24-month-old child is at a critical stage. If a child of this age is introduced to the artificial means of applying two-dimensional activities through a screen to three-dimensional manipulation of an actual activity such as stacking blocks, they will struggle when they actually play with blocks. We need to teach them how to solve problems through trial and error in three dimensions. When the process takes longer to find a solution, it will also teach children the important skill of delayed gratification. In addition, children who use screens for these 3-D activities face additional risk of screen addiction.[7]

To avoid screens and for Lilly's best shot at learning, we created an environment of learning in our home, and consequently, Lilly spent time building puzzles, creating Lego towns, and conjuring up horse communities with her Stablemate horses and barns. As a family, we played card games, built puzzles, and watched movies. Lilly spent beautiful days outside with the neighbor kids, sometimes for more than four to six hours at a time on summer days. She also attended local summer camps and opportunities that opened her eyes to new experiences.

In third grade, Lilly began to show an interest in science. I had been tutoring a few kids from another homeschool hybrid called Living Science Academy (LS). This school's model of education has a different style of teaching than other schools or even homeschool co-ops. They meet one day a week for a two-hour lab, and there is a focus in STEM (Science, Technology, Engineering, and Math). I attended an open house at LS to learn more about the school for our Goddaughter who was eleven at the time, and the owner asked me about Lilly. I explained that Lilly was only going into fourth grade. Their programs started with fifth grade. The owner said she had allowed a fourth grader or two into the fifth-grade class, so she wanted to interview Lilly. The interview went well, and my eight-year-old daughter had the opportunity to be in a class of ten-year-old children. I prayed. Although I didn't get a clear answer from the Lord, I didn't get a closed door either. I decided to tell Lilly about the opportunity, and she was so excited. She had heard about trips they take as well as overnights at the zoo. I still wasn't sure on the first day of school, but she flourished, so my mind was set at ease.

One afternoon in fifth grade, on the ride home from school at RCA, Lilly seemed a little agitated. Finally, she could contain it no more. "Mom, I need to go to another school," she blurted out.

"Why?" I asked.

"The kids in my class aren't as serious about their schoolwork as I am, and I need more."

"Okay, any ideas?" I said.

"Yes, I want to try Gilchrist's Classical."

"Okay, let me look into it."

First, I wanted to look into what had happened that day. I called the teacher, and she explained that during a test, the teacher was called out of the room. Apparently, the students were so rowdy that Lilly got up, went into the principal's office next door, and sat down to finish her test. When the teacher returned to the class, she scorned the students then noticed Lilly was missing. She went next door, and there she was completing the test. Lilly handed it to the teacher and walked back into the classroom. The teacher agreed with Lilly; the class behavior was just not up to Lilly's standards, and it might be best for Lilly to move on.

I know what some of you might be thinking; Lilly is some kind of over-the-top smart kid. She is smart, but that really wasn't it. She has always been an older soul, even though she was only nine when she was in fifth grade. We had raised her to make decisions that can have good or bad consequences. She loved school and learning, and because of her passion for education, we were able to include her preferences in educational decisions. Her being part of the deciding factor gave her skin in the game.

Her choice to be in Gilchrist's Classical School was the greatest challenge of her lifetime thus far. She took her coursework very seriously, and even though she wanted to quit at one point, she clung to her decision and completed the program.

The classical school she chose was intense, I am not sure I could do it today, nor am I sure I would understand all that she learned. Prior to her decision, she had a few friends that attended this school, and she liked what they had to say about it. As a four-year program, the owner met with the fifteen kids once a week for five hours. The interview was intense. He came to the house and spent three to four hours with us and assigned Lilly writing. She would disappear into her room and come back with a written paper. When the invitation came for her to attend the classical school, she was so excited.

The homework looked like something from a university syllabus. It focused on helping students create a foundation using research and study to see that all classical learning is woven together. Lilly's subjects in sixth grade were history, Bible, literature, writing, Latin, and debate. Every week, there were three to five papers to write, a chapter in history to read (by the way, this was the same book from which I was teaching high school history), several scriptures to read and sometimes memorize, a novel to read (for a total of thirteen novels during the school year), a Latin chapter (I knew nothing about Latin, so she taught herself with the CD that came with the curriculum), along with historical memorizations. Some of these memorizations were quotes from old English stanzas from literature. Other quotes were from important documents, like the Declaration of Independence, or from the words of Patrick Henry's speech.

When Lilly was eleven, she struggled as she moved into year three of her program. She had trouble organizing and speaking her thoughts. She didn't want to finish the homework, memorize any quotes, or participate in class. After a few weeks, we asked her if she wanted to continue. She said she was going to get through the year, and we talked about how we could help. Although she did finish the four-year program, she called it the worst struggle of her time in school. But now as an adult, she recognizes that those years taught her how to be tough, do the research, seek the truth, and find her voice.

Lilly never entered the doors of a traditional school. This choice was a prayerful one for us, Lilly included, as it should be for any parent and child. As a parent, however, you also have to ensure your child is preparing for what God is calling him or her to do, and sometimes that means changing the way you do things. You will need to ask God for guidance and direction. What does He need your child to know for the future He has planned for him or her? If the school he or she chooses is not one that you think is a good fit, ask your child why he or she thinks God is leading him or her there and listen.

If you're going to allow your children to have choices with consequences, then they have to be able to verbalize their decisions. Pray that God speaks to you and your children through His Word on big decisions so that both of you are on the same page. Please don't turn to Google for the answer—the world does not have the answers you are looking for. The good news is that the Word of God does!

Hard decisions are just that—hard. But we have to learn to trust that God is speaking to our children even when they are young. The Bible has examples of young adults in adult situations. David killed Goliath between the ages of thirteen and fifteen, Mary gave birth to Jesus at thirteen, and the boy who shared his fish and loaves is thought to be about eight. God speaks to our children if we have raised them to hear His voice. You may be asking yourself, *How do I know what is right for my child?* The question to ponder is not, *How do I know what is right for my child?* The questions to think about are, *What is God asking me to see, that He created within my child? What am I supposed to nurture through opportunities in education that will allow my child to fulfill God's calling?*

Also, don't believe the lie that you have to keep doing things the way you always have. As long as your child is still under your care and under eighteen, it is not too late to make changes that will allow your child to participate in decisions about his or her education or his or her life for that matter.

As a high school teacher, my heart breaks when I ask my students about their dreams, and they have none. Unfortunately, my experience tells me that seventy-five percent of my students don't know what their dreams are. We would be wise to ask our kids the following questions when they are elementary school age:

"If you could be anything, what would it be?

"Do you know how to become a _____ (whatever their answer is from the previous question)?"

How can mommy and/or daddy help you see what it would be like to be a _____?"

Keeping these answers in mind will enable you to find ways to help your children see their dreams in action at the appropriate age. For example, if your child wants to be a fireman, take him or her to a local fire station. If your child wants to be a CEO, find someone who is willing to allow you and your child to visit their office for a couple of hours. Encourage your children to start looking into occupations as soon as they are interested, and then make a path for them to try it out or see it in action.

Helping your children discover answers to the questions about what they want to do when they grow up can lead to more questions. Your part is to stay in God's Word and ask for His help to show you out-of-the-box solutions. As I've mentioned, your child needs to be involved in picking what education is best for him or her, especially as he or she approaches the teen years. If you don't agree with his or her decision, ask yourself and God if there is a reason you don't trust your child's suggestion. For example, if your child were to tell you he or she wants to be in the circus, not only is that idea telling you about potential direction, but also it could be telling you he or she needs to be entertained during the educational years. So, a solution could be to try an arts school or to make sure they are enrolled in an activity like an aerial or trapeze fitness class that gives them a taste of the desired experience.

For high school, Lilly chose to continue her education at LS. She loved her friends there, and some of them had been together since fifth grade. After being a part of Gilchrist's Classical School, Lilly could handle anything academically that they threw at her. One of the unique programs at LS is the Servant Leadership Program. This ten-hour-a-week commitment trains ninth to twelfth graders how to be not just leaders—but servant leaders who lead like Jesus did. Each science class has three to five servant leaders who are knowledgeable enough to teach class if necessary. The students also create a week-long field trip for the high school and the middle school at the beach, where they serve as the teachers, counselors, and creators of the curriculum. There is a contract that each student signs, and the administrators suggest that each student earn the $500 fee instead of the parents writing a check. Lilly worked a summer job that paid for her servant leader program.

In the contract for the servant leadership program is a clause that made these high-school-aged kids stop and think—the no dating clause. This clause is written to help students understand that each job has rules for a reason. The school's reason is that going on these trips meant late nights with little sleep, close quarters, and not a place for hiding out with someone of the opposite sex. During Lilly's time in the program, many students broke this rule, but not Lilly. She understood what a contract meant. She made the choice to abide by her signature and her word that she would avoid dating relationships during the school year.

Choosing Singleness

This choice not to date was one that encouraged another choice: to be happy with singleness. Lilly and I have spent much time talking about how the church places their focus on the subject of marriage and sex to those who are single instead of focusing on who you can be in Christ with or without a spouse. When she was younger, she would tell me that she wasn't going to be as old as her dad and I were when she got married. We just laughed, because while we were older, we knew it was all about God's timing, not ours.

My mom constantly gave me the lecture that I was supposed to let the boy win at games and act helpless so he could be my knight in shining armor. But my dad had another plan. He wanted me to never rely on a man to do anything. He wanted to educate me on plumbing, car repair, and electricity. These conflicting messages were confusing for me, but I chose my dad's philosophy. I came from a small town where practically my whole high school class was married by twenty-one. Dating for me, like Lilly, was difficult because I am very confident in who I am. I traveled alone, moved to new places for my career alone, and walked through open doors without the baggage of a relationship. Just before I met my husband, I was content with being single, and I thought I would remain that way for life.

When Lilly was in high school, she began to feel insecure about not having a boyfriend. I encouraged her to keep moving forward in her own life, following God, and becoming who He wanted her to become. I reminded her that God has the perfect person who will come alongside her as she moves forward rather than stop her in her tracks.

Helping Our Kids Navigate Controversial Issues

One of the difficulties with being a parent who is intentional about raising kids to focus on God's target is teaching them how to deal with the world around them. When you use the term, "education," it would be best to include not just a biblical understanding of issues but also to share an opposing view. This understanding of an alternate point of view will help kids grow up and live in the world with others who don't understand the Bible or with those who reject it. For example, educate your child not just about creation but about evolution as well. Don't tell them what to believe, but instead, help them learn how to research and then watch them find the answers using both "theories." Help them create a conclusion they can stand on.

When a topic is divided, sometimes among church members, expose your children to both sides and let them decide about their own beliefs. Don't limit your kids' access to the information needed because you are afraid they will choose a different point of view than you hold. They need to know both sides to effectively communicate their beliefs. If they don't see both sides, you will be creating a bubble that will humiliate them at some point. There are few things worse than thinking you have good knowledge about something only to find out just how ignorant you are in front of your peers.

Empowering Our Kids to Make the Tough Choices

One of the biggest lessons we learned by letting Lilly make education and everyday activity decisions is that her freedom to choose earlier gave her more confidence to make more difficult choices later. When Lilly was sixteen, she had to decide if she could afford the monthly board at the barn to keep her horse and pay for car expenses including gas and insurance to help get her around to other commitments, including soccer. She loved her horse, Sassy, who had been on loan from a friend. I too had a horse on loan, Minnie. Lilly and I rode together several times a week. This was our time together in the woods, just the two of us, enjoying God's creation. I found it touching that she included me in the pros and cons of her decision. She said, "Mom, would you like an extra three hours a day, three days a week back in your life?" She was talking about the time it took me to drive her to soccer practices, which was more than forty-five minutes each way, added to the ninety-minute practice itself, during which I would grade papers while I waited for her to finish.

In the end, Lilly made a very adult decision to choose to be responsible for her car expenses so that she could drive herself, which meant we had to send our horses, Sassy and Minnie, back to my friend who had them originally. Lilly understood that she was choosing the new experience (driving herself to soccer) over the familiar (riding horses), and therefore, she owned its consequences. We were proud of Lilly and her decision, which was a turning moment for her from childhood to adulthood. We cried together as we waved goodbye to the horse trailer at sunrise, when my friend drove the horses away.

Also, for her to drive herself, we required that she learn how to check the car fluids, change a tire, and what to do in case of a wreck. Thankfully, she hasn't needed that last one. Another new responsibility we gave her was to make her own doctor's appointments and to attend them alone, as long as there were no serious issues.

This process of empowering kids to make choices is how maturity is built, both for children and for parents, who need to know their children are ready for adulthood. Decisions like the ones I've mentioned helped us as parents to trust Lilly's judgment. By starting her out young with making her own choices, she grew into a young adult, and we began the process of preparing for release.

Takeaway Transformation Tips for Parenting Our Arrows

- Our response to our disobedient children needs to be straightforward and quick. Delay stirs up strife and begins to build a wall in communication from both sides. #beawarrior

- We have to learn to trust that God is speaking to our children even when they are young. #helpthemfindfaith

- What is God asking me to see, that He created within my child? What am I supposed to nurture through opportunities in education that will allow my child to fulfill God's calling? #beawarrior

- Your part is to stay in God's Word and ask for His help to show you out-of-the-box solutions. #beawarrior

- This process of empowering kids to make choices is how maturity is built, both for children and for parents, who need to know their children are ready for adulthood. #helpthemfindflight

Chapter Nine

STRAIGHTENING THE SHAFT: DISCIPLINE

My son, do not despise the LORD'S discipline,
and do not resent his rebuke,
because the LORD
disciplines those he loves,
as a father the son he delights in.
Proverbs 3:11–12 NIV

The arrow maker or warrior begins to straighten the arrow by removing notches to encourage a straight trajectory. Then with the same sharp object used to clear the bark, the arrow maker will slowly begin to make the shaft straight. Fire can be used to get out the little bends, but too much fire will damage the wood and make it dry and brittle. Removing little thin strips of wood slowly makes the shaft smooth. To finish smoothing the shaft, the warrior will choose two stones, gently held in one hand with the shaft between the stones, the maker will turn the shaft while moving the stones back and forth eliminating the last rough edges.

You and your spouse are also like the stones—the two rocks in the hand of the Master Warrior. You will work together as one to help your children grow past their rough edges. Both of you guide your children gently forward and back until they feel complete in their childhood journey. This sharpening is part of the disciplining process given to us by God.

What is the Purpose of Discipline?

> You can discipline without love, but you can't love
> without discipline. —Joby Martin, *Anything is Possible*[8]

What is the purpose of discipline? God uses discipline as a mechanism to instill wisdom. With our foundational understanding of right and wrong, which we have learned from belief systems and experiences, we define what actions in our children's lives will need discipline. Discipline is the negative consequence of their actions, and it can be adhered in different ways. It should, however, always be done with love and compassion. All of us have heard of spanking, timeout chairs, and grounding, but have you heard of creative application? Creative application is correcting the wrongs and making them right. (We will review a couple examples later in this chapter.) God's discipline in our lives helps us better understand how-to live in God's world, God's way. The discipline of our children will help them do likewise. After all, they will need to hear God's voice and respond to His discipline themselves when they are ready.

Before we continue, I'd like to make a distinction between discipline and consequences. Although the words are similar, they do not have the same meanings. Discipline is training or doing something to create a specific character or pattern of behavior. Discipline is imposed by others—their rules and direction teach a specific response to an action. Consequences, on the other hand, are the response to decisions any person makes that create self-discipline. These consequences are how an individual learns from choices. A person's choice to not follow the rules laid down by someone else may include consequences because that person made the choice.

In Chapter Five, I mentioned having a plan for discipline and how important it is to define right and wrong with your spouse. Before we had kids, Bill and I looked at the discipline each of us experienced when we were growing up. Making a list of rules and appropriate disciplinary actions if each rule is broken is a good way to have a record of your discussion. It doesn't mean the discipline of your children won't need some adjustment once you get to know them. Many of the rights and wrongs you will discuss won't appear in the actions of your children until they are three or four years old. As parents, however, we must be on the same page when it comes to discipline, or we will send the wrong signals to our children. If one parent is lenient, he or she is like a good cop, and the other, the one who administers the discipline, is like a bad cop. Children will use these delineations to manipulate parents to get the best result for themselves. The following scenario is one in which a child is manipulating his parent. Imagine that a ten-year-old boy goes to his mom and says, "Mom, Dad said it would be okay to go to Tommy's house if you say it is okay." And then the child goes to the dad and says, "Dad, Mom said it is okay for me to go to Tommy's house if you say it is okay." While each parent thinks they are affirming the other, what actually happens is that neither parent has communicated with the other, and you both have just been played by your child. When children manipulate and we as the parents don't communicate, it makes it harder for us to exercise authority and discipline.

Because of maturity level, I've found that third grade is about the right age to ask your children to participate in ideas for consequences. If you and your spouse agree with their suggestions, create a written contract with your children. This contract should contain the ten commandments (reminding them that even as adults we have rules to live by), and then have your children add other rules that pertain to your family community. Make the wording simple so each child can read and understand the rules. Each rule should contain the consequences received if the rule is broken. You as a parent will be held to this contract as well. Holding yourself to these standards is another opportunity to model to your arrows that we all have rules. They will also possibly see that we all make mistakes. This contract will also help them learn, if enforced, that there are consequences to our choices.

A Lesson in Discipline

> He who withholds the rod [of discipline] hates his son,
> But he who loves him disciplines and trains him
> diligently and appropriately [with wisdom and love]
> (Proverbs 13:24 AMP).

This verse reminds us that discipline in love is important for growth of children because it helps them understand that choices have consequences—both good and bad. It is important to discipline your children. Discipline shows them right from wrong, helps them have boundaries, feel love, and grow in the ability to focus.

Like in the process of straightening the shaft, you need to discipline in small bits. You need to know your child's responses well enough to know what type of discipline works. If you put him or her in time-out and there is a healthy response with an apology, forgiveness, and correction of the wrong, then you know that type of discipline—time-out—is working for your child. This knowledge about the best approach to discipline for your child will come with trial and error. Pastor Bruce Frank of the Biltmore Church in Ashville, North Carolina, says, "If you're so caught up in what you can't control, you'll miss what you can control."[9] On an arrow, sometimes you use a tool and other times you use the fire. But you have to be careful not to use too much fire or you will scar the wood. The same carefulness is true in disciplining children.

When Lilly was a toddler, my mom told me to use Lilly's age to reflect the number of fingers I should use to smack on her hand when she was told not to touch something. I would hold up one finger at the age of one and I would gently smack her hand. We increased the number of fingers using up to four fingers at the age of four to get her attention, and she learned when not to touch something. But for the strong-willed child who won't listen, you might want to find a timeout corner. Pick a place where you can see your child, but he or she can't see you. Having your child face a wall will eliminate distractions. Use a timer, but not one that he or she can hear. Little ones have short attention spans, so start with two minutes. If they remain in the timeout chair, you can call them over and have them apologize for their disobedience. If they don't stay in the timeout chair, add a minute every time they get up. Once they are obedient and ask forgiveness, forget the incident. Never recall a child's mistakes once he or she has apologized and resolved the problem. When we ask for forgiveness from God, our sins are removed and forgotten as far as the east is from the west. We would do well to mimic this kind of mercy with our children's sins.

> At the time, discipline isn't much fun. It always feels like it's going against the grain. Later, of course, discipline pays off bigtime, for it's the well-trained who find themselves mature in their relationship with God (Hebrews 12:11 MSG).

To make our discipline effective, we first had to prepare our daughter for it. We had already explained to her that consequences— both good and bad—come from our individual choices, and we were quick to discipline her if she made the wrong choice. As I shared in the last chapter, discipline needs to happen immediately for it to be effective. Small children are absorbing the world around them like a sponge. If part of that journey will get them hurt, then you have to be there to discipline them immediately, or they won't know what the discipline is for. Touching a hot stove, sticking something in a socket, or crossing the street requires an immediate response. Hearing from you BEFORE a potential consequence from one of these harmful situations happens allows little ones to learn a three-step process that will save them: stop, think, and then choose their response. In a way, you are building a pattern in those three steps that will help them make better choices in the future.

Good consequences come from good choices, and to help instill those good choices, God may bless us for them. We as parents would be wise to do likewise and bless our children for good choices when we are able to do so. To show Lilly the benefits of serving others in our home, I placed three jars in the window with a roll of dimes in each. If her father or I did not put away our clothing or items, she could help by putting our stuff away and then move a dime for each item from our jar to hers. It wasn't long before she was picking up everything trying to get all the dimes. Eventually, she collected most of the dimes, which meant she not only served her family, but also, she was blessed with a little reward.

When we had to discipline Lilly for bad choices, we soon learned that she did not like the timeout corner. She preferred spanking over the timeout chair when she didn't listen, because she didn't want to miss out on any activities that we were doing when she was confined to her timeout chair. If we asked her to pick up her toys, we would give her three chances, then we would apply discipline. She would beg for a spanking because that was quick and over. She could then apologize, accomplish what she was asked to do in the first place, which in this example was pick up her toys. But if we put her in the timeout chair, she would have to sit for a few minutes, apologize, and then pick up her toys, which took longer. Then she would miss whatever we as a family had planned until she put up her toys. We decided to use the chair for a quick response to being disobedient. Let's look at other ways God uses discipline in the Bible to give wisdom for better living.

In Matthew 5:23–24, Jesus tells us that we must correct a wrong with a brother before we present an offering to the Father. So, shouldn't we teach our children to correct their wrongs so that their lives will be peaceful within the family? Many times, the wrong toward a brother is a lack of forgiveness. We cannot just right a wrong, we need to ask forgiveness or give forgiveness. Think of the weight lifted when you correct your wrong so that your heart is pure before the Father. When Bill and I read Matthew 5:23–24, a seed was planted that we should teach our child the consequences of respect for people and their things that God has provided.

Here's an example when we taught Lilly a lesson about respecting our things. One morning after I had been in the bathroom, I came into the kitchen to see lovely pencil art on the wall. Instead of time-out, we handed Lilly a rag and cleaner to scrub her drawing off the wall. She cried through the whole process, but she never wrote on the walls again. Then she apologized for her actions. We explained that it was not her wall to write on and that it is important to respect other people's belongings.

James says, "So whoever knows the right thing to do and fails to do it, for him it is sin" (James 4:17 ESV). Teaching your children to do the "right thing" when nobody is watching is called character. And since God expects each of us to be a person of character, it is important that we teach our kids to begin practicing good character. But how do you teach character? You model it. If we do not model character, we are teaching our children to sin, and I know that is not the heart of most parents. A simple way to teach good character is picking up trash when you see it. God tells us in Genesis that we are stewards of Earth, so we should keep it clean. It doesn't matter whose trash it is; we pick it up and put it in the trash to be a good steward.

As I said before, every child is different in the way he or she responds to discipline, and you have to find the one that will help him or her see regret and ask forgiveness like the Master Warrior asks of us. The Bible is clear that discipline is a show of love, not just a bad consequence, if done consistently with wisdom. As we said before, but it is worth repeating, "He who withholds the rod [of discipline] hates his son, But he who loves him disciplines and trains him diligently and appropriately [with wisdom and love]." (Proverbs 13:24 AMP)

Teaching right from wrong
In a world with fewer and fewer morals, how do we teach right from wrong? We check God's Word. When I was a kid, the Ten Commandments hung in every school and courthouse. These commandments are:

1. You must not have any other gods before Me.

2. You shall make no idols.
3. You shall not take the name of the Lord your God in vain.
4. Keep the Sabbath day holy.
5. Honor your mother and your father.
6. You shall not murder.
7. You shall not commit adultery.
8. You shall not steal.
9. You shall not lie.
10. You should not be envious of your neighbor or what he has.[10]

In the Ten Commandments, God is so specific about what is good and what is evil. In another passage of scripture, Paul speaks about another way we can tell right from wrong.

> Do not be conformed to this world, but be transformed by the renewal of your mind, that by testing you may discern what is the will of God, what is good and acceptable and perfect (Romans 12:2 ESV).

If we allow society to teach our children right from wrong, then we allow the world to define who they are. Our children will then miss the truth that, in God's eyes, they are beloved. So, to love your children is to teach them right from wrong using God's Word. Without the truth of God's Word, we are asking our children to carry unnecessary burdens because they are trying to make adult decisions without an understanding of what differentiates good and evil. And then, sometimes if our children choose wrongly, we shun them for choosing the world's idea of good. How do we help them remove these burdens? We turn them toward Jesus, who reminds us in God's Word that He is here to lighten the load. As He says:

> Take my yoke upon you. Let me teach you,
> because I am humble and gentle at heart,
> and you will find rest for your souls.

For my yoke is easy to bear, and the burden I give you is light (Matthew 11:29–30 NLT).

Many parents do not understand Jesus' reference to "my yoke," but for me as a horse person who has worked with trainers of pulling horses, this picture is clear. The way we train a younger horse to pull a carriage is to yoke or attach the younger horse to an older more experienced horse who is also attached to the carriage. The older horse will teach the younger horse how to respond to the driver's commands. There is a physical connection between the two horses that allows the older horse to communicate with the younger. This instruction between one generation to another is critical and should be used within our families. The stories of past generations help us understand where God has guided our families the way the older horse guides the younger. Next, we will now look at how to pass on these stories to our children.

Takeaway Transformation Tips for Parenting Our Arrows

- But how do you teach character? You model it. If we do not model character, we are teaching our children to sin, and I know that is not the heart of most parents. #helpthemfindflight

Chapter Ten

INHERITED SKILL: SHARING THE LEGACY

Children are a heritage from the LORD, offspring a reward from him (Psalm 127:3 NIV).

We all have a story to tell, and hopefully, those who have gone before you shared their stories with you. Most family lineages include those who chose difficult paths and those who chose God's overcoming direction and led a peaceful, prosperous life. Reading about both a biblical heritage from the Lord and learning about other aspects of family history may help both you and your children understand that you likely have a mixed lineage of God's blessings and perhaps some other influences as well.

The search for my heritage meant looking into word-of-mouth stories about Native Americans, who were friends with my family in the Ohio Valley. It also meant reading about Daniel Boone, who famously cut the first road thru Kentucky to the Ohio River called the Cumberland Gap. In addition, it meant learning about the Brothers Grimm, writer brothers whose fairy tales include *Cinderella* and *Little Red Riding Hood*. These stories have been told to children for generations before my Lilly.

Yes, I have been told that I'm related to all these people. While still in search for the proof, the possibility of the truth is found in the research. You might not think you have a divergent history in your lineage like I do, but you never know until you do the dig.

CHILDREN ARE LIKE ARROWS IN THE HANDS OF A WARRIOR

As a high school history teacher, I require that my American History class dive into their family histories. They have a whole semester to look up their ancestry, interview family members during holidays, and record or write stories that many have never heard before. Whole families are surprised about what they learn and from where they have come. We live in such a transient world that today many people don't know the names of their families, much less the cultures and origins of their heritages. It sends them on a great adventure, in which the parents sometimes get more excited than my students. Either way, I am happy to open the door to the chapters of the past using great tools such as Ancestry.com, which is free at the library, and Familysearch.org, another free website. I also use local archives that house great information and news articles that my students would have never seen about their ancestors if it weren't for their assignment. Discovering the strength of these students' forefathers has given them a new outlook on their lives, and many times, it has encouraged them to move forward in difficult circumstances.

As a child, I spent hours with Granny, my momma's mom. She was a joy and a light in my life. I thought she and God were on face-to-face talking terms as a kid because God would send her dreams that sometimes were premonitions. She had six children plus other wanderers that would show up at the dinner table. The shack, as Granny's homestead was lovingly called, was always open to those who needed a meal. From my momma's description, there was never a dull moment. Granny would fill my dreams with stories of my momma as a little girl with all my aunts and uncles and the shenanigans they were involved in. As I reached adulthood, and after Granny had passed, I started diving deeper into the stories she had told me. Sifting through pictures revealed more and prompted me to do additional family research. Thanks to a cousin, I received part of Granny's diary. I loved seeing her handwriting, and I giggled at her sixteen-year-old self.

On my dad's side, I was blessed with a genealogy book that was written by my great uncle for a class in college in the 1960s. In it, he had written what was called "The Ramblin's." Those were stories he wrote as he interviewed my great, great, great aunts and uncles. The accounts relayed date back to the early- and mid-1800s when my family members lived in close proximity to Native Americans. Lilly loved it when we would read these stories over and over again. They become even more meaningful to her because she knew she was part of that lineage. Those stories were full of survival and serving the community. She loved sharing the accounts at school, and history became her favorite subject—just like it was for her dad and me.

God tells people in the Bible multiple times to write down what He did. After all, where would we be as Christians, if those who He commanded to write His works down, didn't? I have kept a journal off and on since my teen years. We write Christmas newsletters, not just to share with our friends and family abroad, but as a record of God's provision and grace in our lives. Each year in January, I write a longer document where I give more detail, or add other parts of our year, along with a prayer for what the next year will bring. I am sort of a family historian now for both sides of the family, and I love putting books together for family members as gifts. I have made cookbooks that contain recipes from my mom's family and pictures of the family at Thanksgiving enjoying those recipes through the years. I have also made "life books," which include written words from a funeral as well as pictures of the loved one and their family members. I have a birthday album, a Christmas album, and a travel album. They are not all complete, but as I add to them each year, Lilly loves to go through them and remember. Please don't get overwhelmed with planning and making all of what I suggested here. These examples are just what we did over time. If one of these ideas excites you, try one of them! Keeping a favorite family picture from the year and a page of what happened can be plenty to let those in the future, get a glimpse of what your family life was like.

Making history with your children is important to help them develop their personalities and learn about the world around them. Plan trips and events that will widen their experiences and show them different cultures. We took Lilly to war reenactments, Renaissance Festivals, drive-thru zoos, Indian Pow Wows, and national and state parks for hiking and camping. The world is your theater, and it is time to get out and explore.

Drive to a local state park and enjoy the lakes and waterfalls around your area. Many of the experiences only require minimal fees. In many states, if you join the state park's association, those fees are discounted or even free. An impromptu afternoon with friends and a picnic at the park or lake can be great fun. Look on the computer for free experiences, such as live outdoor bands during the summer, Shakespeare in the Park, or cultural events like a Greek or Japanese Festival. Peruse your city's calendar and add events that sound like fun to your family's calendar so you can plan as a family to not only attend but also to volunteer in your community. From parades to turkey trots, and from Memorial Day presentations to campaigning for the next city council member, we took Lilly to whatever events our town sponsored and exposed her to great people and fun experiences.

I also want to encourage you to get your family involved in writing down stories they have heard or participated in that will create a family book that can be printed with pictures and then share them with one another. Getting everyone involved helps round out the perspectives about an event, and the collaboration brings a greater depth to the information captured. We all need to know the important history that shaped us into who we are in Christ and how God has moved in each of our lives. Create an account that you and your family members can share in Shutterfly or Mixbook, and let everyone, even the children, participate in choosing their favorite story of the year.

Another fun activity is to create a jar filled with questions for the grandparents to answer about their lives. Make a special notebook where you can either tape or write the questions and have them write in their answers with a special pen. You could also type the questions and their answers later, add some pictures, and print them on the pages of a book. Ask questions like "What was your favorite Christmas gift you received as a kid and why?" "Where was your favorite place to play?" "Tell me about your favorite pet." You will create a wonderful book of stories to read at bedtime or share with the whole family.

Takeaway Transformation Tips for Parenting Our Arrows

- Making history with your children is important to help them develop their personalities and learn about the world around them. #helpthemfindlove
- We all need to know the important history that shaped us into who we are in Christ and how God has moved in each of our lives. #helpthemfindlove

Chapter Eleven

PREPARING THE FLETCHING: TOOLS IN THE TOOLBOX

For God's gifts and His call can never be withdrawn
(Romans 11:29 NLT).

Although many believe that the feathers, called the fletching, make the arrow fly faster, it is actually the opposite. The arrow has a fletching that consists of three same-sized feathers, neatly combed in the same direction. The tops of the feathers curve in one direction toward the back to optimize the flight of the arrow. The feathers are evenly spaced around the shaft and adhered with pitch and sinew near the back end of the arrow. The fletching adds drag and aids the arrow in recalibrating its flight. If an arrow isn't flying straight, it will experience drag from the fletching. As the arrow moves in flight, the fletching offers a resistance in the opposite direction of the turn to keep the arrow on target.

I consider the "fletching" of a child to be his or her toolbox. This toolbox is filled with multiple tools—skills—that you as the warrior will teach your arrow to help him or her fly to the right target. We wondered what Lilly needed in her toolbox…We watched her so we could start preparing our daughter's fletching.

What you help your children learn as they add to their toolbox will help them recalibrate left and right as necessary to stay on God's target. Without this variety of tools, they might fly, but eventually they could miss the target.

As parents we tend to put OUR tools in our children's toolbox, thinking OUR experiences are enough for them to know how and when to use those tools. When we compare our strengths and weaknesses to those of our children, we limit their learning experiences. Take the time to watch and see where your children are strong and encourage them in those areas. When they are weak, explain that it is okay. That weakness gives them an opportunity to ask for help, and it gives you a chance to receive help as well. Teach your children that asking for help is not adding to their weaknesses, but instead, let them know that they are giving God a chance to use others as a blessing. In return, you and your children will get to use your gifts, talents, and experiences to bless others by sharing your collective tools in the proverbial toolboxes.

We all, however, have both good and bad tools in our boxes. In addition to teaching your kids to use their good tools, be prepared to help your kids pull out the bad tools (tantrums, manipulation, and lying, etc.). Experiences may add to the toolboxes, so give them many experiences—both for you and your children. I think the saddest tool I see as a teacher is the instilling of parents' fears in their children's toolbox. God exhorts us to fight fear. His Word says: "God did not give us a spirit of timidity, cowardice or fear, but [He has given us a spirit] of power and of love and of sound judgement and personal discipline [abilities that result in a calm, well-balanced mind and self-control]" (2 Timothy 1:7 AMP). Your fears limit confidence in your children and cause them to put their confidence in you rather than God. Notice again how Timothy says, "God did not give us a SPIRIT of fear" (2 Timothy 1:7 NIV, capitalization added for emphasis). Fear is a spirit, and by allowing your fear to limit your child's experiences, you are giving your child permission to let that spirit in. Once that spirit is given permission, your child loses the power, love, and self-control necessary to hit the target God has created for them.

If your own fears have contributed to your child missing the target, take heart. This misguided trajectory can be reversed. You need to face your fears in front of your children. If you are afraid of heights, take your kids to a zip wire or ropes course and spend the day conquering your fear. Both you and your child will come home with more strength and confidence to face the next challenge God has for you. If one of your fears is things that crawl, take a trip to a zoo, and learn about snakes and insects. Experience handling the creatures that scare you and let your child see you overcome that fear.

Sports, Any Sport

One great way to add tools to your children's toolbox is team sports. No matter what the sport, they will learn skills such as communication, dedication to a cause, and how to work well with others. Avoid the participation trophy because competition encourages delayed gratification and the benefits of hard work. Sports will also teach them how to encourage others and the importance of learning to lose gracefully. One day, when Lilly was about eight, her soccer team won a tournament, and everyone on the team was presented with a medal. Something clicked with Lilly. When we returned home, Lilly went through her room and removed any trophy she did not earn and asked that we take those trophies to the Salvation Army. When we asked why, she said those aren't real trophies. It was one of the first signs of maturity that I can remember. I wish that kind of maturity was all I saw in the realm of children's sports.

Unfortunately, some parents display their worst side on the field of their children's sports teams. I am not saying you can't be excited, disappointed, and yell at the ref every once in a while. Lord knows I did. Just don't be rude about it. As a coach, I had many talks with parents who thought they understood my plan and strategy for the game, and yet most had never even played the sport. In every game, I tried my best to let every player play, even if just for a short time. If a parent didn't see their player on the field during the whole game, he or she thought I was a bad coach. Undermining the coach defeats the purpose of playing on a team, and your attitude as a parent toward the coach becomes your child's attitude toward the coach. God has a purpose for each experience, and the sports experience tends to be the place where the players are the most embarrassed by their parents. Don't be that parent.

The Beauty of Alone Time

One of the tools many of us lack is how to be happy alone. It is hard to learn how to "be still and know," (Psalm 46:10a NIV), if you have to constantly be entertained by someone or something (like your phone). I am a sanguine person, which means I am an energetic early riser, curious to a fault, creative, optimistic, and spontaneous. I naturally prefer to be around others instead of being alone. I remember how difficult it was for me to learn how to enjoy my own company. I was in my teen years before I saw the value of being alone, recognizing how it rejuvenated my spirit and made me want to rejoin the world with new life and vigor. Teaching a child how to be okay with being alone can be a long process, but it is an experience that will definitely be helpful and necessary at times as they get older. I've said this before, but it's worth repeating: Do not use video games for entertainment! Your child's alone time is a time to learn, process, and enjoy the quiet times of life. Use puzzles, trains, Lego®s, building toys, books, and anything nondigital to encourage imagination. Start with a short ten to fifteen minutes of alone time. Don't share with your children that you will be using a timer. If they come out of their room, be prepared with another activity to send them back. Coloring books or Shrinky Dinks, which are plastic pieces to draw and color on with special markers that you can then put in the oven to shrink, were always a hit at our house. Add five minutes of self-entertainment every couple of days for your kids, and eventually, they will find activities they enjoy by themselves. Our daughter could spend hours reading stories to her stuffed animals, building Lego® towns, or playing the piano and singing.

So Many Tools, So Little Time

As I've said many times in this book, your time with your child at home is short. Those eighteen years will fly by, so be selective. Pick the tools that will help them the most throughout their life. Many tools you might not have in your own toolbox, so learn together. My parents taught us so many things. I am not sure they realized until we were adults how much we watched them and followed suit. The biggest lesson was how to deal with people. Being kind and responding in a way that makes the other person feel special is what my parents modeled for us daily at the guest ranch. Your children are always watching you, so learn to respond appropriately, and they will learn well.

It is best to start filling your child's toolbox with the everyday tools. Manners come to my mind. Once children are feeding themselves, teaching them manners is so valuable because eating properly at a table can make a big impression on those around you. For example, the first manner Lilly needed to learn was not to be demanding at the table. It just so happened that when Lilly was little, we only found one book that had a character with her name. The book was called, *Chicken Fingers, Mac and Cheese...Why Do You Always Have To Say Please.*[14] The beautiful thing was that this gem of a book taught the importance of table manners, especially at restaurants. From how to use the silverware to ordering their own food, this book helps children see that manners show you care enough about the others at the table to not be the center of attention. Quietly using utensils, chewing with your mouth closed, passing both the salt and pepper (my husband told Lilly they were married), and using words like "please" and "thank you" are great places to begin as you teach your child table manners. Being able to carry on a conversation over food will prepare your children for life situations like going out on a date, having a job interview, or being socially appropriate at other formal gatherings.

At our house when we first approach the table, I sit down, and my husband stays standing. He then helps me push in my chair, exhibiting manners. He also facilitates meaningful conversations with deep, thoughtful questions. It makes me laugh when I think of all of Lilly's friends and the faces they would make when they heard the topics that we shared at meals together. Some would jump right in with answers, and others were not sure how to participate as we discussed or engaged in banter on various topics. They did not know how to engage in conversation or understand our sense of humor. Sadly, many of her friends did not have the type of open conversations we foster at the table with their own families. These kids did, however, enjoy coming over to our house regularly to hear the topic of the day.

Next, let's discuss other practical skills that also fall under the category of manners. Answering the phone, shaking hands, speaking to an adult, and how to respond to questions are practical skills that nobody teaches anymore. My husband and I didn't know these skills were lacking in children today because we were both taught how to do them at a young age, and we simply applied them in our parenting. But the more we interact with other parents and children, we see that today's children—and even some parents—are indeed missing some of these skills.

Although answering the phone has changed since everyone has his or her own phone, it is still important for children to know how to answer someone else's phone. I taught Lilly to say, "Tammy Largin's phone, how may I help you?" Your children may not use this skill often, but it is still good to know.

When I teach life skills classes after school as a club, the first week is about how to introduce yourself. I make two circles of students: one on the inside facing out, and one on the outside facing in across from another student. I teach them first to introduce themselves by name. Then, I teach them to reach out with their right hand in confidence, give a firm grip with three pumps, then release. I tell them, "No flopping wrists as if you have your hand kissed like a girl during the Renaissance, no hulk grips putting your guest on the floor in pain, and no holding hands after the three pumps, because that can make a person very nervous." The students are a little weirded out at first, but eventually they see the benefits of the exercise.

As parents, we are constantly asking our children what they are doing, but how many of you who are parents have shared what you do, meaning your occupation, with your kids? If you can talk with them about what you do, you will also be empowering them to learn how to answer questions and you will be giving them confidence to talk with adults. Helping your children know and understand age appropriately what you do for a living not only gives them an answer to a question they are asked numerous times as they grow up, but also it shows that you have included them in your world. Students who know the answer to this question in my high school classes tend to show more family connection. Unfortunately, only about one in ten actually know or understand what their parents do for a living.

Responsibility Building

As Lilly approached second grade, we added various activities including making beds, washing clothes, sewing buttons, and swimming. In fifth grade, we added bathroom cleaning and window washing. We moved the skill level up with age. At twelve, she asked if she could take babysitting classes. Those courses included CPR and infant care, and because of these skills, she had a great career in the neighborhood. She formed a strong work ethic from babysitting and those skills.

Lilly wanted a job outside of the house at fifteen, and she found one with a friend of a friend. The job she chose was influenced by an earlier experience. When Lilly was thirteen, she suffered a soccer injury. During her physical therapy, she became interested in becoming a physical therapist. Seeing her interest, I reached out to everyone I knew, and at fifteen, she landed a job at the desk of a physical therapy office. After a year there, she decided it wasn't the physical therapist she wanted to be, but the office manager. She loved meeting with the people, supplying the needs of the staff, and keeping the schedule. This experience not only gave her a chance to see what a physical therapist does, but also, it opened the doors to something she never knew existed. She was working with the responsibility of a young adult, not a teenager.

What is a Teenager?

Here in America, we tend to label people ages thirteen to nineteen teenagers, yet you never see this word in the Bible. In biblical times, children were considered adults at thirteen. Various celebrations in different cultures have marked the entrance in adulthood, including the Jewish Bar (boys) or Bat (girls) Mitzvah, the Hispanic Quince Nera for girls at fifteen, or the Brazilian Sateré-Mawé for thirteen-year-old boys. I think we as Christians need to think about how to bring up our children as adults and skip the word "teenager." If you enjoyed your teen years, you may be thinking, *Are you crazy?* To share why I think we should do away with the term, I want to share more history of the word teenager and its purpose.

"Teenager" didn't come into use until the progressive movement in western cultures. Starting in 1894, the word "teener" started being used. It then became Americanized to "teenager" in 1922. But the term really didn't take until an article in *Popular Mechanics* used the term in 1941. This new term was latched onto by many marketing people who saw a new class of people to whom they could advertise. Someone had decided "teenagers" were a "distinct class of humanity." In the book, *The Rise and Fall of the American Teenager*, author Thomas Hines refers to fourteen-year-olds as "inexperienced adults." What a great description! According to Hines, parents looked at the young adult as going from a mouth to feed to someone who helped support the family. As we moved from the traditional classic education of reading, writing, and Latin and Greek in the 1920s, new classes emerged such as typing, bookkeeping, and home economics.[11] The Great Depression of the 1930s is when students started staying longer in schools, since job prospects were dwindling. Being in school longer meant that the primary influencers in their lives moved from parents to peers, creating, according to Jon Savage the author of *Teenager*, a new untapped market.[12]

So, let's review: God refers to our children ages thirteen to nineteen as adults, but the world refers to them as "teenagers." People in this age group, then, became more influenced by peers instead of parents or figuring out things on their own as adults.

We have seen how this changing of roles of people ages thirteen to nineteen has played out in our own lives. Many of us would never want to revisit middle school or high school as a student. Add social media, gender choice, and political upheaval to the mix, and you can see that Satan is after our children's identities. As we discussed earlier in this book, God always starts with our identity. He calls us His "beloved." We want our children to remember who they are in Christ, and most of all, we want them to remember that they are loved.

Satan wants to replace this identity in Christ with comparison, ridicule, and defeat. He wants to distract our children from their created purpose. He wants to cover their eyes from the promises God has for them, and to take away their innocence. Satan hides their God-given identity to slow the development into adulthood, and he tries to take away the importance of learning responsibility—and sadly, sometimes their parents haven't helped. How can we expect our children to know how to make adult decisions when they are on their own at college, if, under our supervision, we don't give them practice time?

None of us as parents are going to meet the standards of producing what the world says is a perfect arrow. But as Christians, we can still do our best to help our children fill their toolbox with the skills necessary to hit God's target.

As a high school teacher, I see many unfinished "arrows"— students in my classroom. Some of their shafts have been sort of straightened by one parent, but because they feel abandoned by the other parent, there are little notches, and the exterior is rough and raw. If they have two parents in the same household, although this situation is becoming more rare, I tend to see a little straighter, smoother shaft, but the fletching is still in chaos.

While we, as the warrior, want a perfect arrow whose fletching consists of all three feathers straight and neat, we must remember that God is the only perfect creator. Our job is to do our best to help our arrows find the tools that will enhance their chances to fly straight. Some of my students have at least one straight and neat feather (these students have some of the basic tools that make it look like it is all together on the outside, and from a parent's perspective their job is done). With this feather, a student might fly out of the nest somewhere, but there is no trajectory for them to hit a certain target because it is combined with unfinished feathers. The next feather on their shaft may be crumpled (this type of student has tools in a couple areas of life, but flounders in others). He or she knows how to look for a target associated with what he or she is good at but has no guidance on how to get there. Another possible feather can be either hanging by the sinew or missing completely from the arrow (This type of student is still cognitively a young child with little or no tools in their toolbox, no parental involvement, and they are barely hanging on). Other students have too much parental involvement, so there is no fletching at all and it's as if the parents don't believe their students need any tools of their own. Therefore, the student is expected to fly on their parent's fletching hitting their parent's target, not God's.

Regardless of the state of their fletching, these students have thought little about life, much less dreamt about the future. They have not been allowed to make any choices on their own that would lend themselves to the trajectories of their futures. They have been told what school to attend, beginning with kindergarten up through college. When they want to get a job, they are told that their work is their schoolwork, so they never learn how to manage money or time. These arrows with little previous independence have no concept of how to care for themselves because they have never been taught how to do chores, cook a meal, or do laundry. My heart breaks when they tell me that right and wrong are relative, and they are to focus on themselves rather than the importance of community and serving those around them. They have no tools in which to make adult decisions, yet their parents dump them at the college of THE PARENTS' choosing and assume their college age students can somehow manage their own lives. Then the parents of these young adults are disappointed when these arrows spend too much money, get sick from burning both ends of the candle, or get involved with the wrong crowd to feel accepted.

As their teacher, I do my best to explain that the reins to THEIR futures will need to be in THEIR hands. I tell them they need to "own" their futures, find courage, and be willing to have tough conversations with their parents so that they can ask them for the reins. Telling my students that they are old enough to make life-changing decisions is foreign to them.

Telling them to get a job so that they can save their money to buy their own car and pay their own insurance seems like an impossible task in their minds. Many have never been trusted to do anything of value that would add to their self-worth.

So please, I strongly advise you to NOT follow suit of these students' parents, who may have not known better. But you, reading this book, have the benefit of learning from others' difficulties. Give your kids simple tasks such as cooking, cleaning, and laundry. Give them the chance to see that life is full of necessary small jobs that make the big ones go smoother. Encourage your kids to participate in their community. Very few of my students have had any responsibility growing up, and therefore, they don't know what the word means. These are great young people, who should be experiencing the beginning of adulthood, but instead, they lie beneath the decay of no decision-making skills.

As we have seen, the "normal" treatment of many teenagers in the last century is actually the opposite of biblical wisdom. Timothy tells the youth in the church to "Let no one look down on your youthfulness, but rather in speech, conduct, love, faith and purity, show yourself an example of those who believe" (1 Timothy 4:12 NASB). If we are not the encouragers of our children's gifts, skills, and ideas, they will turn to their peers for support. Instead of finding support, this lack of encouragement will, in turn, create chaos in their souls because their minds, souls, and spirits are in flux. The messages they receive range wildly between being treated as a child and trying to learn how to take on the responsibilities of an adult.

In addition to confusion, this lack of affirmation creates anger and hostility for people in this age range toward the authorities in their lives. This rising anger because of lack of affirmation especially affects young men. As you likely know, your boys are watching the men in their lives. You will see them mimic the way they dress, walk, and treat others. If you are a single mom, please pick wisely who you want your son to mimic. Dads, think about how your boys perceive you. Pay attention to the way you treat your wife daily. Think about how you respond to her needs. Show it is okay to cry when you are sad or hurt. Embrace your boy or young man with hugs that show the love and compassion of the Father. Be the dad you wanted growing up and seek the Father for answers that you might have never received as a young man.

Give them responsibilities so they can show you that they are maturing in their lives. As the warriors, we can clear up the confusion of what it means to be an adult by taking proactive measures. Allowing your child to start a small business, even at the age of ten, shows creativity, leadership, and a desire to serve the community around them. Babysitters and pet sitters are always needed in the neighborhood. Your children know they are coming into adulthood. They are looking for the opportunity to show that they can be responsible and earn their keep through a job or skill.

I'd like to share an early success story. My second cousin started a lawn business at age ten. By twelve, he owned his first bounce house, adding it to his lawn business. He hired his dad to help with delivery and set-up. By fourteen, he operated four bounce houses every weekend. That young man made enough money to pay cash for a brand-new half ton pick-up truck when he turned sixteen. This year, he graduates from high school. He has added construction equipment, like front-end loaders and ditch diggers, pushing his income beyond what most college graduates make. Bringing in this amount of money sent him looking for a way to contribute to his community. He bought a small bus, and today, he transports children and adults to and from events and church free of charge. All of his older siblings have their own businesses, and none of them have college degrees. I attribute the success of this family to the parents, who worked alongside them as young adults instead of viewing them as teenagers. These parents helped their children embrace their business ideas, and those ideas became reality.

The Technology Dilemma

As I've mentioned, even though Bill and I both worked in technical fields, we did not allow Lilly to have any technology or video games as a young child. As I've also shared, before Lilly was born, I owned a small company that provided afterschool computer classes in the public school computer labs. We taught kindergarten through fifth grade students how to use a computer. We pulled computers apart, taught typing skills, and showed kids how to do homework using software like Kidpix, Microsoft Word, and PowerPoint.

During that season of life, I found that so many of my young students came through my classes so hooked on the computer or computer games that parents didn't know what to do with them. The parents I interacted with at that time would ask if I would speak on behalf of my experience with their child when counselors would request that they be evaluated for ADHD. Most of these students were good kids who needed another venue, like recess or a swivel chair, so they could keep the wheels turning in class without causing a scene.

Our children are not wired to sit still in a classroom, hours on end, without a break. Heck, as adults we aren't wired that way, so why do we educate our children this way? Most children don't know how to sit and enjoy a rainbow, how to patiently wait for a fish to bite the hook, or how to find solace in just sitting in God's beauty for more than thirty seconds. How are they going to learn how to wait on God, hear His gentle whisper, or feel a light breeze if everything in their lives is instantaneous?

We gave Lilly her first phone at fourteen, out of necessity. We had an extra cell phone as a home phone for emergencies and when she traveled on school trips. We told her it was not a toy; it was a tool. No gaming or social media apps were allowed. No computer was allowed, except for schoolwork. Life for her was about, well...life. She went outside to explore, enjoyed watching frogs and playing in the mud. She rode her bikes with friends and played imaginary life games like house and school. Unfortunately, so many parents have forgotten how much those imaginary life games increased their skills for life.

Those of you who grew up in the era I did may remember the neighborhood kickball game, for which all the kids would gather in the cul-de-sac and play until our parents made us go in for dinner. Those in-person community activities are what many kids are missing. We picked teams, encouraged our friends, sorted out arguments, and despite whatever went on, we couldn't wait until school was out the next day to play another round. Our parents didn't get involved in the solutions; we worked our problems out. From those situations, we learned about communication and hopefully compassion for the last person picked.

Tools Need to Be Interchangeable

A tool that works in one scenario can also work in another. A simple example is tying knots. Learning to tie a knot is a skill that is widely used. From tying shoes to putting a tarp on the bed of a truck to keep the rain from getting your stuff wet, most of us can tie a knot. Showing your children various knots with names is probably something you might not have learned as a kid, but you could have used a thousand times. I encourage you to learn together.

Painting is another great example. Start on a canvas and work up to painting the walls of your child's room. And do it together. Painting builds relationships, and you can learn so much from the conversations that you may have as you work. You can also have fun singing songs together from Spotify or Pandora and spontaneously break into a dance. When you are done painting, you can both have pride as you stand back and look at a job well done. There are many more interchangeable life skills you can do together. Ask your child to make some suggestions and then jump in and do these activities together.

Although various tools are what help us play a sport, pass a class, or get a job, none of the tools in the toolbox work if we don't have the knowledge to use them.

Knowledge is a funny thing. Did you know we learn more from failure than from success? Success can be deceptive and give us a false sense of security. Why would I say that? I think God planned it that way. If life was all success, we would have no need for God. He wants us to know that the only one true secure place is in the arms of Jesus. We need to fill our children's minds with knowledge and help them learn how to teach themselves to apply that knowledge, using the tools they have been taught, so that they can gain wisdom. In other words, we need to teach them how to fail successfully. *WHAT?*

In preparing my lessons as a history teacher, I've found that many great inventions and companies have come into existence out of previous failures...M&M'®s, Bubble Wrap®, Super Glue, Play-Doh those are just a few, but the list goes on and on. Yet look at the success of these products today. We have heard sayings like, "Failure is just a step on the way to success." "Without failure there will be no success." etc. And although these statements are true, it isn't the success that was successful. It was the attitude of the people who were in leadership at these companies. They learned from their failures and then moved forward. They didn't use their failure to keep failing; they pressed on to the higher goal, not forgetting that the failure could also be a success in its own way. I've noticed that many parents must not be teaching their children this perseverance. The pervasive sentiment instead seems to be that everything is disposable. If it breaks, we throw it away instead of fixing it. For some children, if they feel broken, they think they are disposable as well. This attitude is not acceptable.

Just like my dad taught me, my husband and I tried to teach Lilly all the essentials of life: how to do basic car maintenance, how to clean a sink drain, how to change a light switch or outlet. I also added the incredible gift of YouTube. Teach your children the basics of using tools, and they can learn anything. Now that Lilly is an adult, she has a little house, and she is quick to find solutions to the problems that arise. It is not just a quick phone call to a handy man. We raised her to apply herself to any problem. And thanks to YouTube, she is quite successful!

Tools are meant to be used, and like any skill, your knowledge diminishes if you let your skills lie dormant. If you teach your child how to use a tool, then he or she needs to use it in a timely manner. Don't step in and solve all their problems for them, or you will never see them fly. Remind them to apply their knowledge to every challenge God puts before them. Your children's knowledge is about using their minds and working with their tools, but another component is essential: their hearts. You will need to focus on shaping knowledge—the shaping of the minds, some of which we have discussed—and dealing with emotions or issues of the heart, which is what we will look at next. Molding both of these areas create a sharp arrowhead that can penetrate others with the Gospel.

Takeaway Transformation Tips for Parenting Our Arrows

- Teach your children that asking for help is not adding to their weaknesses, but instead let them know that they are giving God a chance to use others as a blessing. #helpthemfindflight

- Your children are always watching you, so learn to respond appropriately so they will learn well. #helpthembecomeawarrior

- We need to teach them how to fail successfully. #helpthemfindflight

- For some children, if they feel broke, they think they are disposable as well. This attitude is not acceptable. #helpthemfindlove

- Don't step in and solve all their problems for them or you will never see them fly. #helpthemfindflight

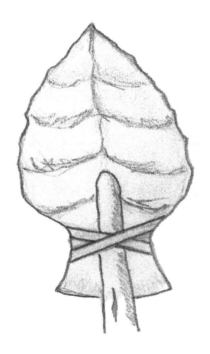

Chapter Twelve

CRAFTING THE ARROWHEAD: THE HEART AND MIND OF A CHILD

> A good man brings good things out of the good
> stored up in his heart, and an evil man brings evil
> things out of the evil stored up in his heart. For the
> mouth speaks what the heart is full of
> (Luke 6:45 NIV).

The arrowhead is the most important part of the arrow. Its purpose is to penetrate flesh. Our arrowhead analogy is the representation of the heart and mind of the child.

I strongly recommend that God's Word be your guide as you craft your child's heart and mind. We used scriptures to speak truth as we prepared our arrowhead. One way to ensure His truth sinks into your heart so that you can pass it along to your child is to read God's Word out loud to your children. You might be using your own voice, but His Spirit is filling your heart and mind with God's breath—and if your children can hear you, He is filling their hearts and minds too. They, in turn, at the proper time, will be penetrating those around them with God's truth.

Conversely, an arrow without a good arrowhead is just a stick bouncing off the target. This arrow could be represented as the "ME focus" of society, which has created lonely, depressed, anxious, non-participating citizens. God did not create us to focus on ourselves, but instead, He wants us to look at Him and those around us.

CHILDREN ARE LIKE ARROWS IN THE HANDS OF A WARRIOR

> The LORD God said, "It is not good for the man to be alone. I will make a helper suitable for him" (Genesis 2:18 NIV).

Although this scripture was originally about how God created a spouse for Adam, I believe it is also telling us to all be a "helper" to all of those around us. As humans, we were not created to be alone and without help. How do we teach our kids to have servant hearts and caring minds? We turn to Jesus as our example.

> "...whoever wants to become great among you must be your servant, and whoever wants to be first must be your slave— just as the Son of Man did not come to be served, but to serve, and to give his life as a ransom for many" (Matthew 20:26–28 NIV).

This passage tells us that a God-designed arrowhead-shaped mind is not programmed to focus on the best schools, the highest paying jobs, and the picture-perfect American dream. This arrowhead is focused on the truth from the One who gave us life, serving the creation of those in His image, and learning how to receive God's provision for well-being.

We relied on God to provide our every need, and Lilly saw Him bless us with more than we needed so that we could bless others. Lilly learned, from example, how to jump in and serve the homeless—not to get a selfie with them as some her age did. She saw us providing for others in need with solutions to help them with their problems rather than just feeding them for a day. Knowing Him and His truth, then applying it, feeds the arrowhead-shaped mind God is looking for in us, as warriors in training, to craft with Him, the Master Warrior.

> Our children and their children will get in on this. As the word is passed along from parent to child. Babies not yet conceived will hear the good news—that God does what he says. (Psalm 22:30–31 MSG).

Let's go back to our study of making arrows to glean additional understanding about how to best shape the arrowhead. The stone chosen for the task of being transformed into an arrowhead is aged, beaten down, and weathered by rain and heat. The stone is then buried, and a fire is placed over it to prepare it for knapping, which is the process of removing excess stone to make the arrowhead sharp for penetration. The stone has purpose, but the arrow maker will need to help it find its best shape for a razor-sharp edge. The stone will not change shape unless it gives way to the arrow maker. The arrow maker warrior must be patient, using bone and other tools he will carefully remove stone little by little as the arrowhead takes shape.

To help steward the hearts of our children, we need to show them how we penetrate the hearts of others by sharing our testimonies. Therefore, we need to allow our kids to be present and hear it. As we give our testimonies, we need to be sure to share the compassion of Christ to those who are listening. When we do so, our children will want to do the same. They will want to know who it is that gives us this compassion to turn the other cheek, use words gently, and give to those in need.

We need to also share the good news about Jesus with our children. We need to read straight from the scriptures about His way, His truth, and His life. Jesus said, "I am the way, the truth, and the life. No one can come to the Father except through me" (John 14:6 NLT). Our children need to know that they need to be born again. Jesus said "Truly, truly I say to you, unless one is born again, he cannot see the kingdom" (John 3:3 ESV). Without getting too theologically deep, part of what the kingdom means here is having eternal life and perceiving what Jesus did to save us and what the Holy Spirit still does to bring Heaven to Earth to overcome evil. If you are a Christ follower, your highest hope should be to see your children receive the rebirth this verse speaks of—salvation. Helping your children find out who God is and guiding them to a relationship with Him creates the weapons needed for the warfare that awaits them.

CHILDREN ARE LIKE ARROWS IN THE HANDS OF A WARRIOR

As we have discussed, we are in a spiritual battle, and there is an enemy that wants to defeat us. In Romans, Paul reminds us, "Therefore I urge you, brothers and sisters, by the mercies of God, to present your bodies as a living and holy sacrifice, acceptable to God, which is your spiritual service of worship" (Romans 12:1 NASB). Satan wants us to think that giving all to God as a living and holy sacrifice is weird and unnatural, yet by not choosing to give all, we are choosing the world. So many parents have lost their sense of who provides for them and who they are to worship, especially if they have lost their jobs. Instead of worshiping God and trusting Him to provide in a new way, we may realize—especially when we have material losses—that we have been worshipping big homes, fast cars, and luxurious vacations. We need to change our example to our children. We need to give thanks for provision, fight the battles of this world on our knees, and remind both ourselves and our children that we know from where our help comes.

Paul continues in Romans 12, "And do not be conformed to this world, but be transformed by the renewing of your mind, so that you may prove what the will of God is, that which is good and acceptable and perfect" (Romans 12:2 NASB). Transforming ourselves and rubbing off on our children is our hardest job as a parent. We see our mistakes, our bad choices, and the directions we took when we were children, but our children are not us, and they need to experience life to make good decisions. Also, we are still transforming daily, and so are our children. They will continue to transform as they leave the nest and for the rest of their lives. Our kids have to be part of their own transformation process so that they know how to receive transformation from God once they are out on their own.

As you lead your children on their own spiritual journeys or in practical life skills, ask God daily what needs to be removed from your arrowhead stone to make it stronger, sharper, and more focused on its goal WITHOUT crushing it. New arrow makers crush a lot of rocks before they get good at their craft. But they are not consulting the Creator while they make their arrows. (If they did, they would likely not waste as much rock!) You will need to have a path to God that will be well traveled. BUT I HAVE TO WARN YOU: As a parent, do not try to remove the world without the child's consent. Our children must be a part of this process. Like a baby bird emerging from an egg, this process of chipping away the world is one that will add strength to the warrior within. Each chip and scrape, made together through prayer and love, will help the child grow closer to God. We will need to start loosening the apron strings so they can begin to test their new-found weapons on their own. This loosening of the strings doesn't mean our job is done. Our children need to see the choices in our lives that make us different from their friends' parents. Leaning into God for all decisions, picking that path that starts on our knees, and asking our children questions will help them make decisions on their own instead of us as parents dictating their futures.

If we look at each of our children as a raw stone, we will see that no two stones are exactly alike. This uniqueness is important to remember as we are sometimes told by supposed experts that children have to fit in a particular assigned compartment. My heart breaks thinking about how different Lilly's life would have been if we had listened to these experts. Even at birth, she was compared to other children of her age. I got a lecture from my pediatrician about weight, vaccines, and cognitive ability. They wanted to assign her a certain percentile. Then it was time for school, doctors tested her and put her on an educational scale, testing for ADD, ADHD, and other alphabetical labels. I couldn't do it anymore. My personal opinion is that we diagnose the quirky, the different, and the oddities way too early. God wants us to see these things and live with them so that we will seek Him about how to deal with them. Listening to a diagnosis can be overwhelming and sometimes it drives us to our knees, but for many, it adds a bump to the road that limits what God wants us to see in our children.

For me, I didn't want to rear my child focusing on imperfections, because I knew He made each of us special with different focuses, abilities, creative levels, and physical limitations so that we can complement one another. Unfortunately, some of our societal experts have either forgotten about just how individual each one of us is, or perhaps they are not allowed to treat us individually by the powers above them. With each lecture I received from doctors and others about education, I found myself back on my knees asking God to reveal what He wanted for our child. This constant asking God about our daughter is where the most important intentionality came into play.

She saw us on our knees; we did not hide the fact that we were praying. She heard us read His Word out loud and discuss it at the table, where she too was included to have her own opinion. She saw God's provision in our lives, and we gave Him the glory without hesitation.

As we allowed her to help us remove little bits of rock from her life, we saw God's calling on her. We watched our daughter love people, serve people, and most of all, seek God on her own.

With the shaft straightened and smoothed, the fletching combed and trimmed, and the arrowhead sharpened with an edge to penetrate, these elements will be joined in relationship to one another to form the arrow. God uses relationships, what we will look more at next, as the glue to hold the parts together so the arrow can fly through the battle and hit His target.

Takeaway Transformation Tips for Parenting Our Arrows

- Our children will be penetrating those around them with God's truth. #helpthemfindfaith

- We need to give thanks for provision, fight the battles of this world on our knees, and remind both ourselves and our children that we know from where our help comes. #helpthemfindfaith

- Our kids have to be part of their own transformation process so that they know how to receive transformation from God once they are out on their own. #helpthemfindfaith

- Like a baby bird emerging from an egg, this process of chipping away the world is one that will add strength to the warrior within. #helpthembecomewarriors

- Leaning into God for all decisions, picking that path that starts on our knees, and asking our children questions will help them make decisions on their own instead of us as parents dictating their futures. #helpthemfindfaith

- I didn't want to rear my child focusing on imperfections, because I knew He made each of us special with different focuses, abilities, creative levels, and physical limitations so that we can complement one another. #helpthemfindfaith

- We watched our daughter love people, serve people, and most of all, seek God on her own. #helpthemfindfaith

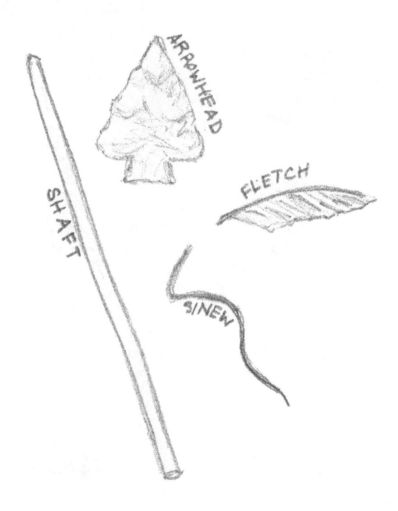

Chapter Thirteen

ARROW ASSEMBLY: BINDING RELATIONSHIPS

Therefore encourage and comfort one another and
build up one another, just as you are doing
(1 Thessalonians 5:11 AMP).

Now that we have all the parts: the shaft, the feathers for the fletching, and the arrowhead, it is time to assemble the arrow using pitch and sinew. Pitch is made from tree sap and used as a glue. In our arrow analogy, pitch represents the common interests that bring us together in relationships—interests like sports, belief systems, occupations, and food to name a few. Sinew is created from the tendons of any mammal. They are the string-like things used to attach muscle to bone. Both have been used for thousands of years to bind items together. While pitch is an introduction to relationship, sinew is the relationship itself.

Pitch, the common interests that draw you to a group of people of like-mindedness, gives you the chance of introduction. This group of people become acquaintances; you begin to know their names, occupations, and family members. From those introductions a relationship may blossom—one in which you reach beyond the small talk and dive into deep topics. In these types of relationships, you encourage one another and hold each other accountable. They are the sinew that holds the parts of the arrow together.

It takes multiple pieces of sinew to complete an arrow, just as it takes multiple relationships in life to become the person God has created you to be. For the arrow, you will use three pieces of sinew:

two for the fletching and one for the arrowhead. After the arrowhead and each feather is glued in place with pitch to the arrow's shaft, we use the sinew to strengthen and support the attachment of the fletching and arrowhead to the shaft. To prepare the sinew, the warrior must chew on it. The saliva moistens the sinew, allowing it to stretch and secrete a glue-like substance making it sticky. To adhere the sinew to the arrow, we lay about one half inch of sinew on the shaft starting just before the fletching. Then, we begin to wrap the sinew tightly back over itself and the fletching end, each time being careful to not overlap the sinew but keep them side by side for multiple wraps. This process will adhere the fletching in place. The sinew is secured by feeding it back through the wrap with a needle. The arrowhead, after being glued with pitch, is attached differently with a crisscross wrap over the notches of the arrowhead and around the shaft for a secure attachment. As the sinew dries, it will begin to shrink, creating a tight bond between the arrowhead, the fletching, and the shaft.

Like the sinew is to the arrow, relationships are the most important part of life. A good relationship consists of many experiences and situations that will increase the bond between two people. Like the wraps around an arrow, the more wraps, the stronger the bond. If we do not make time for relationships with those we love, both friends and family, we lose our purpose for living. Our relationship with Jesus needs to be our first priority. It is the foundation on which all good relationships are built, especially with our families. There would be no arrow if it wasn't for the sinew; instead, we would only have a pile of parts. In the same way, a family without relationships is just a group of people living under one roof.

In the 1970s, a significant shift in typical parent-to-child relationships began that continues to create a chaos and confusion in our country today. This change correlated with a change in discipline for children. This shift embodies the belief that a child should be able to create his or her own boundaries and make family-sized decisions. The result of this shift allows the child to be in charge rather than the parent(s).

As Christians, we know God created the Ten Commandments so that we could live a much more fulfilling life in community—starting with Him and in families. With an instruction to honor the father and mother, it's clear that the child making the boundaries is not honoring the father and the mother. Therefore, these changes were not biblical. This upside-down family hierarchy creates more conflict, leaving the parents to feel somewhat helpless and not fulfilling the role God instilled for them as a steward. Other commandments help children (and all of us) have a standard to live by. Our family is where our children will learn about community as well as how to live in peace with one another. To live in community, we need to teach our children the importance of Jesus' words that are found in Matthew's Gospel:

> Jesus replied: "'You must love the LORD your God with all your heart, all your soul, and all your mind.' This is the first and greatest commandment. A second is equally important: 'Love your neighbor as yourself' (Matthew 22:37–39 NLT).

With the greatest command to love the Lord with all your heart, soul, and mind, we need to teach our children that God should always be our first love. We need to show them that every action and attitude should reflect that we love because He first loved us. Showing our children that God is a good and loving God—and teaching them that He only wants the best for us—helps them turn to Him rather than run away from Him. To demonstrate this principle, we have to be vulnerable as parents. Explain to them that you are learning how to be the parent God created you to be as God is showing our children how to become the arrow that will eventually hit God's target. Relay stories, like the parables of Jesus, that tell the stories of people running to God in times of struggle. Use the stories from your childhood, when you were near your child's age, that show that honesty was the best policy. Tell them about instances of how bad choices led to bad consequences and explain how struggle in our life eventually led to success and reward. Sharing that you are fallible can help a child know that it is okay to NOT be perfect. This call to be vulnerable does not give you license to complain about your situation to your child. Instead, this attitude lets your children see that you rely on Jesus in your every need.

Let your children pray for you because out of the mouths of babes come peace and understanding for both them and you. Teach them to give Him thanksgiving in every turn of life—good or bad—explaining that His plan is so much better than ours, even when we can't see past our curtain of circumstances. Like I said before, raising children is just as much a journey for you as it is for them, so embrace God's teaching for you as you teach your children.

Although Jesus, referring to the commandments, tells us that loving our neighbors as ourselves is just as important as loving ourselves (Matthew 22:39 NLT), actually implementing loving our neighbors can be so much harder. We are born into sin, and we have to remember that our children are not angels. They too have the sinful nature until they personally respond to the call of Jesus. Teaching peace and harmony through loving one another as you would like to be loved takes some practice. None of us are perfect in this area, and you will be tested. So, just hang on, and let Jesus take the wheel when you feel overwhelmed.

Responding to THEIR personality

One of my favorite books that I read when Lilly was a toddler was *Personality Plus* by Florence Littauer. This book helps readers understand that we need to know our own personality qualities to best deal with others whose personalities are different from ours. I found myself asking Lilly questions from the book to help me figure out how to best respond to her personality.

Then when Lilly hit fifth grade, we found another great book, *The Treasure Tree*, by John Trent and Gary Smalley, which helped us see how Lilly's personality fits within our family. I wished we had heard about the book earlier because this book helps children understand different personalities and celebrate each other's strengths. Through the adventure to find the treasure tree with the four friends—the otter, beaver, lion, and golden retriever—the child sees how God creates all of us differently so that we can help one another. After a quest to fulfill her position in our family, Lilly decided she was the otter, which meant she was all about the party. Planning was part of that, and with her beaver coming a close second, she worked hard to make every event meaningful and fun. Time flies! As a matter of fact, as I was putting the final touches on this book, she graduated with a degree in hospitality from the Dedman School of Hospitality at Florida State University. We had no idea that party planning interest, which was nurtured at age ten, would actually become her focus as an adult.

Graciousness Builds Relationships

Because of how we were raised and our research before Lilly was conceived, we knew we needed to be a constant presence in Lilly's life. She needed to see that our homelife reflected Jesus, both at home and on the road. One way we tried to display His love was through graciousness. Another quote I love by Joby Martin of Church of Eleven22 states: "God does not give us everything to be happy because then we will lose the opportunity to be thankful."[13]

Sharing what it takes to run a household with your children and then being thankful when they help with household chores builds their confidence and increases their desires to serve even more. This eagerness does not mean you won't get the usual pushback as kids grow older, but if you stand your ground and remind them that they receive benefits from participating in the family's needs, they will likely cooperate more than they would have without you remaining firm. Also, don't forget to thank your kids when they do things correctly. Want a gracious child? Then model it.

In our household, we have found that being thankful for everything that we do for each other encourages us to continue blessing each other. If my husband does the dishes, I thank him. If I clean the bathroom, he is quick to notice and thank me. If Lilly makes cookies or cooks dinner, we thank her. This graciousness is not only a blessing to those who receive praise, but also, this affirmation builds

129

courage for each family member. It builds courage for us to step out beyond what might be considered normal non-expressiveness in a family unit. It gives us a chance to be extraordinary in how we see God's image in each person we serve—especially our family members.

Our graciousness is one way we have been told that we are different from other families. People actually notice how thankful we are to each other as a family as we serve one another. They notice when Bill, Lilly, and I say thank you, yes/no ma'am and yes/no sir. Some see it as old-fashioned, but in our house, it is a sign of respect and appreciation. No matter the age of the people we interact with, we try our best to be courteous, and with God's help, to also be loving—no matter how we feel in that particular moment. This commitment doesn't come without challenges, but Bill and I both believe that you get what you give. Our friends from England saw us saying yes ma'am and no ma'am as courtesy, and they wanted their children to do the same, but without the southern flare. We suggested "yes, please" or "no, thank you" as a great alternative.

We always try to thank Lilly for the smallest of things. We want her to recognize that we see she is trying to participate in community with us as a family. We were very intentional, because our focus as a family was to serve others in our community and we wanted her to catch that fire. After all, Jesus came to serve, not to be served, and that is our calling as well. Although there are many times that we as families enjoy being together and serving the greater world around us, there are also times that we hurt each other or irritate each other. In those instances, we must also learn to be intentional for the sake of preserving family relationships.

The Art of Arguing

When you have to confront something verbally, there is an art to arguing that helps bring resolution with the least amount of harm possible so that the relationship can be restored. I was not taught this art as a child. Arguments have been one of my struggles, and from many of my conversations with others, I know that I am not the only one. My "go-to" action is to walk away, digest the conflict, and then come back to it later when I have cleared my head. Knowing how to argue is a life skill that you need to teach your children early. Jesus calls us to resolve conflict over and over again to show that we appreciate His forgiveness of our sins. How can we be thankful for our forgiveness if we do not give others the forgiveness needed to release them into the freedom of Christ?

You are going to make many mistakes, so be prepared to ask for forgiveness daily. The beauty of children is how forgiving they can be if you are honest with them. Putting on a happy face in front of your children when things in life are difficult robs them of the experience of learning how to manage being disappointed, sad, or overwhelmed. There were many times that our daughter prayed to God for me in times of distress. Her prayers not only lifted my circumstance to God, but also they were a fragrant incense to my heart.

My husband is an artist in arguing because he can talk calmly in a disagreement and understand both sides of the argument. I am in awe of how he does that so well. He is the one from whom Lilly gets her skills. Bill has often made arguing somewhat of a game. It always started with a word banter over a topic, and then the deep conversation would begin. Therefore, Lilly always felt comfortable bringing anything controversial to the dinner table, where we would discuss these matters. I would start out calmly telling my opinion, but feeling my passion windup, I would eventually silence myself (mainly because I didn't want Lilly to learn to argue like I did which was getting angry or shutting down). Then Bill's calm response and logical thoughts would take over. Although Lilly sometimes refers to these times as "the lecture," she really learned how to see both sides of an argument and pick her beliefs wisely.

If you are like me and don't know how to keep arguing calmly, start praying. I am so much better at arguing because of praying first than I was when we first got married. I have always known I am not good with expression in the middle of a fiery moment. I resort to writing in my journal and then return to the conversation with my husband later.

By stepping away to write a letter to the Lord, I could hear Him better and be better at communicating my thoughts and emotions to my husband. There are times I still need the pen and paper and a little time to organize my thoughts, but most importantly, I am learning to listen to the Holy Spirit and His Word, which says in James, "Understand this, my dear brothers and sisters: You must all be quick to listen, slow to speak, and slow to get angry" (James 1:19 NLT). The words in this verse are ones we need to teach our children. Say them out loud to yourself so they hear that you too struggle with the same difficulty. "I need to be quick to listen." As you make that statement, ask yourself, what was said that caused the pain? Listen for the Holy Spirit's direction. Make sure you heard correctly, not trying to read between the lines, but instead, focus on listening to the person's words. Repeat what you heard to the person to confirm understanding.

Let's talk some more about the words from James, "Slow to speak..." Listening has to do with the Holy Spirit, but speaking also engages Him to speak through you. Most of the time, we tend to lash out, which is relying on our "flesh," instead of the Holy Spirit. Lashing out by reacting too quickly only deepens the hurt. Even worse, we tend to lash out at the people who we love the most and who have the potential to hurt us the most—our family members. Let's stop this behavior! Learn to use the silence within the argument to listen to the Holy Spirit. Like the movie theater message says prior to the feature presentation starting, "Silence is golden." It is golden in an argument as well.

Another strategy to teach your children about how to do well at the art of arguing is how to take a deep breath to exhale the anger that is rising up. "Slow to get angry" is because you are allowing the Holy Spirit to take control of the situation knowing that God has a plan and you do not want to get in the way. To stop the anger from rising further within you, inhale the cleansing breath of the Holy Spirit and exhale the anger that has risen up in the heat of the moment. That pause will help you slow down your heartbeat, give oxygen to your mind for better clarity, and allow the Holy Spirit to step in and defuse the moment.

The Necessary Skill of Confrontational Communication
Learning communication that is not only understood but presented in love is a challenge we all face in the midst of confrontation. "I hate you!" Lilly screamed as she stomped down the hall into her room and slammed the door. My heart was broken. It was then I heard the words in my head, *Sound familiar?* How many times had I said exactly the same thing to God as He showed me something I just didn't want to do. I began to change my prayers as I whispered these words, "Soften my heart, oh God, to not only help this child but to hear her. In this situation, show me how you see me." That prayer was opening a can of worms that I never expected. I knew I was selfish, prideful, and sometimes very arrogant, but God heard me, and little by little, I began to learn so much.

As a daughter of a very strong, southern mother in a family with a business, my arguments as a child, especially during the teen years, were not pleasant. I wanted a different relationship with Lilly. I wanted a relationship that would be compatible and supportive of each other, so I sought the Lord.

An answer actually came through a confrontation I had with my husband. My success in writing in my journal to resolve conflict with my husband led me to begin the same practice with my daughter, which turned more into a note campaign.

I told Lilly to write why she felt that my answer made her angry and was not okay with her. I also told her to slip it under the door where I was working after she was finished writing. I would write back with questions so that the communication was clear. With each note, I learned more and more about my daughter's heart and how she communicated. It could take as many as three or four rounds before the air was cleared, but eventually, we understood one another enough to say what was on our mind without getting offended.

Lilly rarely got in trouble to the point of grounding, but when she did, our decision stood. Grounding for us involved removing all screens (television, computers, and phones), doing manual labor (yardwork or housework without pay), and/or being home bound without any option of attending events such as parties or entertainment with friends. With Lilly, there was no negotiating about grounding. No matter what opportunities arose, the consequences of her actions remained. It was during these moments that I would receive a note under the door explaining why she did the action that got her in trouble. While her confessions came through on a piece of paper with apologies for the action that caused the consequences, the grounding remained because Lilly was not in control of the situation.

These notes helped Lilly and I understand one another. Bill and I did not, however, allow Lilly's notes to become notes of negotiation that changed the original decision he and I set for her discipline. The notes would allow me, as a parent, representing Bill and me, the opportunity to explain our reasoning for our response to the situation.

I'll give you one example. I sometimes made comments to Lilly like, "You only have the family dishes to do, I had a whole guest ranch of dishes at your age." She let me know in a note that this comment was not helpful. Some of the notes broke my heart because my words, even if I had good intentions, brought more anxiety to Lilly, because she was not able to keep up with who I was at her age. I thought I was encouraging her to be happy, because she was only cleaning up after three of us instead of fifty.

After I received this note, I wrote back with a full apology for comparing her to me. These types of incidents reminded me that God has made each of us as individuals with unique strengths and abilities. And although there might have been a few similarities, I needed to see her the way God sees her and stop the comparisons.

Today I have a little box with her picture on it where I keep these notes and other notes of encouragement from Lilly. When I miss her, I return to that box. I cherish them because God used those notes to change me and to help Lilly find her voice. When I need words of wisdom, I reach for my Bible and Lilly's words, which have taught me how to be a better person.

Through these notes, I received so much more than a stronger relationship with my daughter. The Holy Spirit taught me about how I respond to God's direction and instruction. He revealed how my disobedience was completely in the way of my spiritual growth. I was not good at being "grounded"—either as a child by my parents, or by God as an adult. As a teenager I was grounded for disobedience, not coming home at curfew, and other things I have since forgotten. My parents' grounding of me meant that I was not allowed to do outside activities, and extra chores were always added without pay like cleaning windows, the garage, or any other cleaning project that hadn't been done in a while.

Seeking God's Resolution to Conflict

While we were raising a child, we as adults learned more about ourselves and our relationship with Christ than we ever would have without raising her. It helps me to keep God's perspective when I treat each experience that causes conflict as only one specific incident rather than apply it as a lifetime mandate. Will God put a similar experience before us at another time? Absolutely! Will we walk away from this particular page of the journey because we have "been there, done that"? Helping a child think past a problem to a solution is probably the hardest thing to teach our children because we all have experiences that hinder having right mindedness—Holy Spirit mindedness. Belief systems have molded us through family traditions. Church doctrine created from man's view of religion rather than relationship with Jesus has in some ways led us down a path far from the truth of God's Word. Our experiences can be based on a lie that gives false testimony. Using our belief system and experiences, we may try to write our children's story by filling the voids we had as a child, but we have to allow our children to experience and make up their own likes and dislikes. Projecting our experiences on our kids may diminish their budding independence or the journey God has planned for them.

CHILDREN ARE LIKE ARROWS IN THE HANDS OF A WARRIOR

Teaching Conflict Resolution to Your Children

> A man's discretion makes him slow to anger,
> And it is his glory to overlook a transgression
> (Proverbs 19:11 NASB).

Conflict resolution was one of the big struggles for me, and it was from the mouth of my babe that God spoke to me on the topic. Even today, she knows how to get my attention in a conversation. She helps me steer my mind to be more open to what is being said, and then I can respond in questions rather than blanket statements. I have learned that while we are all one human race, our experiences have sometimes led us to be closed-minded to the possibility that we could be wrong. Many of Lilly's friends have come to me for advice through the years. The title, "Mom" tends to lend itself to helping one fix a problem. I have learned, however, that my experience at their age was so different, that I have to change how I think before I speak. Social media, gender identity, and mental illness have all changed how we as parents need to respond to our children.

But how do you relate to your children in a way they can understand and remain a parent to the child in a relationship? I had watched so many of my friends be stepped on by their children, even when they were only two or three years old. These children demanded to be served rather than to do things for themselves. As the children grew up, they just became more manipulative, and I wanted to avoid that. I asked God for solutions.

Between the isolation that began with the pandemic of Covid in 2020, and the social media-based society, some of us have lost the skill of communication. I cringe when I hear parents excited to communicate via text with their kids. Texting is for short quick questions and answers, it is not a platform for relationships. Teaching your children the art of communication is a skill that many of us actually struggle with ourselves. When and how to say something in a way that doesn't elevate emotion is a gift that few of us have, so it is important to find what will work for you and your children. Asking children questions without giving input is a skill as a parent and a teacher that I had to learn. Just listening, without your phone in hand, shows them that they are important. Give children opportunities to vent so that they can share their sides of conflicts to talk through processes or solutions. Your undivided attention shows them that you recognize they are growing up and trying to apply logic to situations they face. We have all likely faced times when we need to rant to get our feelings out. Then someone tries to solve problems for us when we didn't want help, but we just wanted to be heard. As tempting as it is, don't be the problem solver unless your child specifically asks you what you think.

As a teacher, I have seen a switch in how conflict is resolved for our students. Parents seem to be quick to respond when it comes to little Johnny getting in trouble at school, but rather than Johnny apologizing and paying the penalty, a negotiation begins, and Johnny isn't even in the room. Rude inappropriate comments and jesters, missing assignments and unfinished schoolwork are excused away with ball practices, family trips and *"Oh, that's just his/her personality."* If Johnny feels bullied or uncomfortable in any way, the parents swoop in, never giving Johnny a chance to learn how to apply solutions to the conflict.

If Lilly was involved in a situation, she was part of the solution. We did not negotiate deals for her, and we always held her accountable for what was required of her. I can remember a year in middle school science when she received an "A" for the semester from the teacher, and as the parent I knew she had not made an "A." It was a rough year of missing assignments and even missing projects so there was no real "A." We sat down with Lilly and asked what needed to be done on her part to complete the class correctly. We wanted her to understand that nobody gets away with anything, God knows she didn't earn the "A," so she needed to be honest with herself about it. She agreed to repeat the science class the next year.

Another example is a conversation I had with a young mom whose daughter was having trouble with a classmate. They had started out as friends, but then the other girl became mean and treated this young mother's daughter harshly. Rather than encourage her daughter to continue to be friendly and share kindness, this young mom told her daughter to stay away from the other girl, and the mom even confronted the other mother to keep her daughter away from her child. By the time this young mom called me, the "mean girl" had apologized to her daughter and wanted to be friends again. But the mom found herself yelling at her child, saying that she needed to stay away from the "mean girl." I explained that she needed to apologize to her daughter and then explain to her daughter that she needed to pray for the "mean girl." The mom would also pray that Jesus would give her daughter the kindness needed to continue to win the former friend over.

We have to give our children the skills to love beyond the situation, and we need to teach them how to define the line so that they know when to walk away. As parents, we are not present in these squabbles, many of which are just that—squabbles. We all had squabbles as children, and because our parents did not interfere, we learned how to come to the table, negotiate terms, and agree to a solution. I am seeing more and more parents getting too involved in their child's squabbles, and the child never gains the knowledge of how to resolve a conflict.

As parents, we want to protect our kids in their everyday lives, but when we fix every little disagreement, we prevent conflict resolutions skills from developing. We raise children who don't know how to disagree without winning. Many times, when we disagree with our children, we quelch their opinion without considering that their experiences are different from ours.

To help your children find their voices, step back when there is a conflict and give them time to resolve it, but not too much time. ASK QUESTIONS! Failing to ask questions is where we tend to make mistakes as parents. We THINK we have the answers, but our children have not had our experiences (theirs are not the same as ours were).

The right time to give them their own voice is when they face conflict. By asking questions, you can help them think through the process and find a solution, rather than interjecting your solution. If you see a bump in their solution, ask another question, and another, until they see light at the end of the conflict.

Lilly learned much about conflict resolution from a book I mentioned earlier: *The Treasure Tree*. She hated it when her friends fought, and she would appoint herself as the mediator in almost every situation. If the friends couldn't work it out, she came home. The neighbor would call and ask what happened. I would put Lilly on the phone, and she would explain the situation. A few minutes later, the doorbell would ring, apologies would occur, and "Bye Mom" would be yelled as the door slammed shut. I would never intervene, because both my husband and I felt that she needed to know how to stick up for herself—without violence. For Lilly, when she needed to apologize to her friends, sometimes she wrote a letter, and sometimes she bought or made something that she would give to help heal the pain between them. Most of the time it was of her own doing, but asking questions made her find the solution and built confidence that she could face the next conflict on her own. She also learned how to walk away when it is necessary too. Many times, in fact, she did walk away.

While I was watching Lilly grow into the young woman God was calling her to be, the spiritual growth I received opened the door for me to help my high school students better communicate with their parents. I recommended ways my students might use to open up relationships with their parents that once were ignored. I learned that the busyness of life we parents face has left our children feeling alone and unheard, which causes so many to shut down. Therefore, open communication between students and their parents stops—if it ever existed. So, I encourage my students to start conversations and to see if they can get their parents to participate. The fear of rejection is a vulnerability they do not like, but I think they hate the feeling of aloneness more. The solitude can drive them to find relationship elsewhere, unfortunately many turn to the counterfeit form of relationship.

Counterfeit Relationships (Social Media)

We can't have a conversation about relationships and not discuss counterfeit relationships. Earlier we spoke of how Jesus eases our burdens because He loves us unconditionally and He reflects truth. Media, on the other hand—both social and non-social—has the potential to create unauthentic relationships, to damage traditional family bonds that we as parents may try to create, and to cause us to internalize false messages. Therefore, media can increase our burdens. Media of all kinds offer various ideologies that unfortunately have led not just young people, but adults as well, down harmful paths of self-destruction. As we wait for the "likes" from our pithy comments and memes to be tallied, eventually our hearts lose the desire to serve anyone but ourselves. Don't let Satan dictate your child's identity through the influence of the ungodly media he or she may be exposed to.

As a high school history teacher, I see students making wrong choices daily because their influencers on YouTube or social media told them how to dress, speak to a girl, lose weight, or choose their gender through a meme or short. They are led to believe that these ideas presented by influencers will solve all their problems. The disappointment students face when the results are not what they have been told or what they expect can have traumatic effects, some of which are life altering.

Unfortunately, I have had a few students attempt suicide, some of which have been successful, and my heart is broken. Others find themselves connecting with the wrong crowd through chat rooms or getting addicted to drugs and alcohol. I am fortunate that I have been at a school where we are quick to respond, but often there is denial by these students' parents, which makes my heart ache. Satan is such a liar. He will do anything to take the lives of our children, and to not lose any more to suicide or addiction, we need to act now.

Considering how harmful social media is to you, ask yourself, *Should my child be on social media?* If we as adults are affected by the self-focus or destructive disputes presented in social media, how can we blame our children for following the ideas and morals that are represented in social media? They too will want to lose weight, but they won't use a healthy mode to accomplish that goal. Instead, they will use the methods and words of their favorite influencer. The habits they are seeing are becoming their norm, and in many cases, we are doing the same. Therefore, using social media can create a household full of people who are self-focused and have no communication skills. As viewed in the movie, *The Social Dilemma,* most developers of social media do not allow their children to use their creation. That fact alone should be a big red flag.

So, since we know that media is not a good example for our kids in helping them know how to live or who God created them to be, are we as the parents filling in the gap? Or are we allowing teachers, scout leaders, youth pastors, and others to do that for us? I shared earlier that one of our key verses is Proverbs 22:6, in which Solomon tells parents to "Train up a child in the way he should go and when he is old, he will not depart from it." BUT have you read, or do you remember verses 4 and 5? These verses explain why we are to train our children in the way they should go. Let's read the entire passage together:

> The reward of humility [that is, having a realistic view of one's importance] and the [reverent, worshipful] fear of the LORD
> Is riches, honor, and life.
> Thorns and snares are in the way of the obstinate [for their lack of honor and their wrong-doing traps them];
> He who guards himself [with godly wisdom] will be far from them and avoid the consequences they suffer.
> Train up a child in the way he should go [teaching him to seek God's wisdom and will for his abilities and talents],

> Even when he is old, he will not depart from it (Proverbs 22:4–6 AMP).

In this passage, we can see that we train children so that they follow the Lord, which helps them avoid being ensnared.

In addition to training our children on the ways in which they should go, we would be wise to look at our own behavior when we examine these verses.

Have we shown our children who we are in Christ by our example, so that they desire the same relationship with Him that we have?

Our calling as parents is to enhance our children's journey, not limit it. How do you do that? You find like-minded people who become the bow to your arrow.

Takeaway Transformation Tips for Parenting Our Arrows

- With the greatest command to love the Lord with all your heart, soul, and mind, we need to teach our children that God should always be our first love. #helpthemfindlove
- Let your children pray for you because out of the mouths of babes come peace and understanding for both them and you. #helpthemfindfaith
- Teach them to give Him thanksgiving in every turn of life—good or bad—explaining that His plan is so much better than ours, even when we can't see past the curtain of circumstances. #helpthemfindfaith
- Another strategy to teach your children about how to do well at the art of arguing is how to take a deep breath to exhale the anger that is rising up. #helpthemfindflight
- While we were raising a child, we as adults learned more about ourselves and our relationship with Christ than we ever would have without raising her. #beawarrior
- Asking children questions without giving input is a skill as a parent and a teacher that I had to learn. Just listening, without your phone in hand, shows them that they are important. #helpthemfindlove
- Give children opportunities to vent so that they can share their sides of conflicts to talk through processes or solutions. Your undivided attention shows them that you recognize they are growing up and trying to apply logic to situations they face. #helpthemfindfaith
- The mom would also pray that Jesus would give her daughter the kindness needed to continue to win the former friend over. #helpthemfindlove
- We all had squabbles as children, and because our parents did not interfere, we learned how to come to the table, negotiate terms, and agree to a solution. #helpthemfindlove

- To help your children find their voice, step back when there is a conflict and give them time to resolve it, but not too much time. #helpthemfindlove

- The right time to give them their own voice is when they face conflict. By asking questions, you can help them think through the process and find a solution, rather than interjecting your solution. #helpthemfindflight

- One way we tried to display His love was through graciousness. #helpthemfindlove

- Don't let Satan dictate your child's identity through the influence of the ungodly media he or she may be exposed to. #beawarrior

Chapter Fourteen

→→→————————————————→

YOUR BOW:
THE INVESTMENT GROUP

Iron sharpens iron, and one man sharpens another
(Proverbs 27:17 ESV).

Did you ever try to throw an arrow and hit the target? Have you ever stabbed a target with an arrow? Or have you dropped an arrow on your target from a higher place by climbing a tree or a ledge? Envision with me that you are giving it a try. Think about what you would do to try your best to make whatever arrow you have stick to the target. First, you would attach a target to a tree and take a stance ten feet from the target. Some of you would use a paper airplane or dart throwing technique with the arrow lightly between two fingers, opposite hand in the air for balance. You would lunge forward with your body as you throw. You might have hit the target, but the arrowhead does not stick into the tree.

Some of you would hold the arrow with an underhanded fist like a spear. Then you would take a few steps back and then run toward the ten-foot line, releasing the arrow with everything you've got. As you try this method, you might hit the target, but an arrow might just bounce off. With frustration you pick up the arrow, run up to the target on the tree, and try to make it stick by stabbing it in the target over and over, but your repeated attempts end up breaking the arrowhead, and your perseverance leaves a giant hole in the tree. In all these scenarios, the arrow would hit the target with little velocity, and then it would fall to the ground, where it would lie until someone else picks it up. The point of envisioning this scenario is to demonstrate that it is hard to launch your arrow and hit the target with accuracy without the help of a bow.

You are the warrior, but it takes more than just your family to launch a child into the world. Let us create a bow with those we know who are good, godly people to invest in our children. At our house, we called these people the "investment group." God had put them in our path to guide and direct Lilly in her gifts.

God chose five ladies to be Lilly's bow. It is both biblical and important to have investors of the same gender for safety reasons. The Book of Titus is very specific about how younger women look to older women to learn.

> By looking at them (virtuous older women), the younger women will know how to love their husbands and children, be virtuous and pure, keep a good house, be good wives. We don't want anyone looking down on God's Message because of their behavior. Also, guide the young men to live disciplined lives. (Titus 2:4–5 MSG, parenthesis added for clarity).

Our investment group of ladies served as the bow, and they spoke to Lilly about who God was in their lives. They did not tell Lilly who God should be in her life. They had no legalistic rules; instead, they showed the love of Jesus in whatever they did. Their individual behaviors showed Lilly many ways to love people and love God. They were examples of Jesus, and they were willing to take Lilly from time to time to participate alongside. We were and are so grateful.

Lori and Laura served as the directors for the kids' praise team at our church, and they taught Lilly how to pray. That was their ministry—teaching the importance of prayer. They embraced Lilly and all of her questions about praying including, "Where is God when I pray?" Lilly has a deep desire to see God move, and you can see it in her expression as she prays. They also taught her to be thankful with every prayer. She is thankful that she has a God who loves her, and she is grateful that one way He shows her that love is through provision. She has learned to be thankful that God has a plan even if it is not her plan, and she is to be thankful that she lives where she can come to Him without fear of imprisonment, torture, or even death.

Verna is a good friend of mine who had a youth music ministry. Lilly excelled at vocals. We could see her gift of worship, so Verna took her under her wing and taught her not only vocals, but allowed her, at thirteen, to attend an intense Precepts Bible study on worship. She showed her the importance of words, especially those in God's Word. The Bible study demonstrated how He loves us through His Word. As a middle schooler, Lilly found the importance of what God was saying and how He is consistent in His Word. She saw the importance of meeting with God each morning, and how it improved her day if she took the time to get up early and seek Him. She would also write notes to her friends with scriptures that she thought would help them with whatever they were facing. God's Word encouraged her, so she would encourage others.

Kelley was Lilly's small group leader from middle through high school, and Kelly taught Lilly compassion. Kelly taught Lilly and other girls how to love each other even when they were hurt, and in some cases, pointed out when they were being mean to each other. Kelly showed the girls how to love without condition. Middle school is difficult. Everyone is trying to become who they think the world wants them to be, but Kelley's influence of prayer, and just being there for the girls to talk about most everything, gave them a safe space. Kelly taught the girls from a biblical worldview, giving them alternatives to what the world was telling them. And she did it with her sweet, sweet, heart of compassion.

And last but not least, there was Kelle Mac, who taught Lilly how to open her home to those in need. She taught Lilly about being the hands and feet of Jesus through provision. Kelle is what Jesus talks about when He says feed My sheep, give them clothing, and a place to live. Weekly she had a youth group in her home, and there would be up to fifty high schoolers hanging with their friends, learning about

Jesus, and seeing what living a Christian life looked like. Kelle's heart for the lost and broken rubbed off on Lilly. To this day, Lilly carries water, socks, and $1 bills to give to those she sees around her town. Lilly is such an example of what I want to be from the perspective of all these women who took the time to know her and guide her in the ways of God.

We could have never filled the shoes that God provided so readily through these women. They were examples of Christ whose giftings were different from ours. Our child's personality allows her to have different perspectives and experiences than us. She needed other people in her life that love God differently than we did. She needed additional examples of how to find God and His calling in her life. We knew these women were chosen by God, and we wanted the opportunity to let Lilly walk with these ladies. As Lilly interacted and learned from them, she was also honing her skills and relationship with Christ.

We think it is important that you know that none of these women ever approached us. We turned to them after Lilly had attended various programs each of them provided. She came home from these programs desiring more, which opened our eyes to how God was using each of them to show her God's target. So, we asked each woman to spend a little more time with Lilly, and they opened their hearts and their homes. You could say she spent some time in their quivers, but we were the benefactors of Lilly's developing heart when she returned home to our quiver and shared what she was learning.

Takeaway Transformation Tips for Parenting Our Arrows

- You are the warrior, but it takes more than just your family to launch a child into the world. #helpthemfindflight

CHILDREN ARE LIKE ARROWS IN THE HANDS OF A WARRIOR

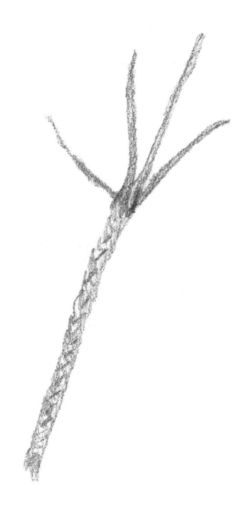

Chapter Fifteen

BOWSTRING: THE HOLY SPIRIT TO YOUR BOW

But you will receive power when the Holy Spirit comes on you; and you will be my witnesses in Jerusalem, and in all Judea and Samaria, and to the ends of the earth (Acts 1:8 NIV).

A bow can only be left with a bowstring attached for a couple weeks before the bow starts to lose shape. The bowstring is tested by the archer warrior for strength, elasticity, and water resistance. Increased twists will be added to the tension of the bowstring for balance of the bow to string ratio and will give them more launching power. A good bowstring at its best will help the warrior perform the shot with distance, accuracy, and speed. During biblical times, a bowstring consisted of linen and hemp, sometimes twisted tightly into a single cord. Although twisting materials is the fastest way to complete a bowstring, this method does not make the strongest bowstring. The strongest bowstring is made using a technique called reverse twisting, which is a braiding technique using four strands of fiber.

In the quest of trying to be as transparent as possible, I want to share that I completely forgot to write about the bowstring in my first and second draft of this book. My overlooking of this important part was a tangible reminder for me of how often we forget the third member of the trinity—the Holy Spirit. The first picture to pop up in my mind was that the four strands were God, the Father; Jesus, His Son; the Holy Spirit; and my husband and I, but then I was reminded once again that this journey was Lilly's—not ours. So, her soul would have to be the fourth fiber of this bowstring—not a fiber that represented my husband and me.

The Holy Spirit, as an extension of Lilly's relationship with God, chose the women I mentioned as her "bow" in the last chapter. And although the construction of the bowstring included all of the Trinity and Lilly, the braided string as a whole—the completed bowstring—in our overall analogy of the parts of the arrow represents the Holy Spirit. The Holy Spirit, just like the bowstring, created the fire power needed to launch Lilly into full adulthood.

At some point, every analogy has flaws. And this one about the arrow leaves out the part of self-determination necessary as a child nears adulthood. Normally the warriors, which in this analogy has been the parents, carve the nocks at the back of the arrows. But a young adult will need to choose to carve his or her own nock. If the nock is carved by the parents, an early release could leave a young adult feeling kicked out of the nest without muscles strong enough to fly. If the nock is never carved, a young adult will fail to launch. As parents, we hope our children carve with prayer and guidance from the Holy Spirit, so that they are prepared to be launched toward God's target.

I was prepared for my launch. My parents dropped me off at college with all my stuff, and although I returned home for school breaks and worked through the summers for the guest ranch, going away to college was my passage into full adulthood. I was ready. My self-determination had me carving my nock months before when my parents moved to another state during my senior year of high school. When they put my belongings in storage near the college I would attend several states away, I knew my flight to independence was not far away. If my mom had carved my nock, she likely would have wanted me to stay close to their new home, and she would have limited the decisions I could make—for my future. But my dad is the one who saw I was ready. I needed to fly. God had showed me His plan, and I wanted to be faithful.

As your children prepare their own nocks, you will see, as my dad did, the maturity through their actions and decisions. Them preparing themselves doesn't always mean the work is completed, it just means they are ready to tell you, the parent warriors, that they feel confident enough to be launched toward God's target.

Our children need to choose to follow Jesus on their own. The bow helped us guide her toward the Lord. She embraces His truth. Lilly has her own relationship with Jesus, one completely independent from ours. Choosing to follow Jesus gave her the confidence to create the nocks for her bow. She began to apply all she had learned from the bow, and she started seeing the Holy Spirit move in her own life. She had been braiding the Father, Son, and Holy Spirit to her soul as she began to carve into herself for the last part of her as the arrow—the arrow nock.

If we, as parents, carve our children's nocks, our arrow will have a hard time when it is time to rely on God's next launch. Although we as Christian parents want our children to have our passion for God and a desire to seek His truth, we cannot force this desire on them. Jesus says:

> Look! I stand at the door and knock. If you hear my voice and open the door, I will come in, and we will share a meal together as friends (Revelation 3:20 NLT).

We cannot open this door for our children; this is one they must walk through on their own. Our example as warriors hopefully shows the possibilities of living a life of freedom in Christ. For those possibilities to be evident, OUR relationship with Christ needs to rise above all others.

As you conclude this chapter, I want to encourage you to take a deep breath, to rest in the Father's arms, and to watch Him move in your children's lives. Some of my friends thought it was crazy that I would ask Lilly if she had time with God every morning. But isn't that what we should ask if we are training them up for warfare? For some reason, we are told by some that our faith is private. But I can't find that privacy in the Bible. What I do find is that we are ALL called to preach the Gospel, and you can't live your faith privately and obey at the same time. In the Gospel of Mark, Jesus tells his disciples:

> And He said to them, "Go into all the world and preach the gospel to all creation. He who has believed and has been baptized shall be saved; but he who has disbelieved shall be condemned" (Mark 16:15–16 NASB).

We are not to hide our faith under a bushel, (see Matthew 5:15), behind your front door, or in our bedroom. As one of the verses we just read in Mark 16 says, we are to "GO." Sometimes going is talking to someone at school or the grocery store; other times we are to go to feed the homeless or we are to travel to Africa. But just like any trip, we need to pack our bags for the adventure. And before the arrow launches, we need to show them how to dress for war!

Chapter Sixteen

DRESSING FOR WAR: THE ARMOR

Finally, be strong in the Lord and in his mighty power. Put on the full armor of God, so that you can take your stand against the devil's schemes. For our struggle is not against flesh and blood, but against the rulers, against the authorities, against the powers of this dark world and against the spiritual forces of evil in the heavenly realms. Therefore put on the full armor of God, so that when the day of evil comes, you may be able to stand your ground, and after you have done everything, to stand. Stand firm then, with the belt of truth buckled around your waist, with the breastplate of righteousness in place, and with your feet fitted with the readiness that comes from the gospel of peace. In addition to all this, take up the shield of faith, with which you can extinguish all the flaming arrows of the evil one. Take the helmet of salvation and the sword of the Spirit, which is the word of God. And pray in the Spirit on all occasions with all kinds of prayers and requests. With this in mind, be alert and always keep on praying for all the Lord's people (Ephesians 6:10–18 NIV).

How do we teach our children to be strong in the Lord so that they become the warriors they were created to be? First, we show them His Word and the power found within. Most American churches try their best to provide the truth of the Gospel to our children, but ultimately it is our responsibility as their stewards to share with them the full power of God's Word. To share something, you have to have it yourself. If you have not experienced His power, ask Him to show you where He has rescued you over and over again. Many years ago, I made a timeline of my life. It was an assignment in a Bible study. God revealed so much to me about His divine providence and how His hand was always there even in my darkest times.

As Lilly approached high school and she was preparing for her launch, I shared my timeline. This exercise goes along with one common discussion I have had with other parents—whether we tell our kids, at an appropriate age, the truth about our pasts. My answer is to share the truth. A warrior in training (parent) from the Master Warrior passes on his or her wisdom to the arrow as he or she crafts it. This wisdom cut into the arrow tells a story of wars won to give strength to the arrow as they prepare for their own flights. I have shared my own experience with Lilly about how God grabbed me when I had strayed and turned my life 180 degrees to become a servant for family, friends, and my community.

Here is a bit of what I told her about this season of my life. Although much of my youth was spent as a good child under the roof of my parents, it was my adulthood that brought me shame. Saved at fifteen, I knew right from wrong, yet being in the entertainment world exposed me to other lifestyles that included drugs, sex, and alcohol. I lived two lives: one wherever I was living, and another when I was with my parents and other family. I wanted Lilly to heed the warning signs, which include ignoring time with God and replacing that time with partying.

Therefore, I told her everything when she was about sixteen. I spoke about how alcohol had destroyed my innocence, taken away my faith, and gave me an "I don't care" attitude about my body and life in general. God rescued me. I finished the story where I took a 180-degree turn, thanks to the redemption of God and a little white church. I told Lilly about the women who laid hands on me and prayed throughout the night to help me find healing from all the hurt. Lilly thanked me for being honest, and I felt God would use my honesty to help her understand the importance of staying focused on His forgiveness and love. She has heard me minister to her friends and others about my experiences and how God grabbed me just in time.

I encourage you to see your journey as one that made you who you are today—a child of God, an image bearer who knows who their Father is. Your experiences—good and bad—are to be shared with your children. They need to see God's faithfulness at work in your life.

> Put on the full armor of God, so that you can take your stand against the devil's schemes (Ephesians 6:11 NIV).

We need to look at this verse carefully. Notice it says to put on the FULL ARMOR. And these words are repeated in verse 13. You can't just put on the helmet and be protected because then your heart is exposed. Your belt of truth is worthless if you don't have the breastplate of right-mindedness. You can't hold the shield of faith and not carry the sword of the Spirit. Your faith needs the Word of God to hold it strong. Don't teach your child about salvation, and then forget to put on the rest of the armor. That is like sending them out to play hockey with just a helmet and no pads. Our children need to understand *all* of the armor, and they need to understand why they need to wear it daily. Do you understand what it looks like to put on your armor daily? If not, give it a try. Put on your armor in the mornings with your children and be confident that your family is protected from the devil's schemes. Schemes is a word that means a secret or devious plan. We don't know what the devil has planned from hour to hour or day to day. So, we need to teach our children to protect themselves, and there is no better protection than the armor of God.

> For our struggle is not against flesh and blood, but against the rulers, against the authorities, against the powers of this dark world and against the spiritual forces of evil in the heavenly realms (Ephesians 6:12 NIV).

CHILDREN ARE LIKE ARROWS IN THE HANDS OF A WARRIOR

One of the hardest topics to teach is that our battle is not with flesh and blood but against the powers of this dark world and the spiritual forces of evil. Nobody talks about evil anymore. It is almost taboo in some churches. But we must talk about it. To start this conversation, explain how sometimes we as adults do things unintentionally that hurt others. Then ask your children if they have ever hurt someone unintentionally. By encouraging them to recognize that sometimes we as humans do things we don't mean to, you are demonstrating to your children they are not always fully aware of how their actions or words affect others. They need to learn how to recognize when they hurt someone and be quick to apologize.

Although sometimes we as humans unintentionally hurt others, our world is also full of people controlled by Satan who deliberately want to steal, kill, and destroy. We see this in the division of our country and churches. Since 2018, there has been a rise in crime and violence, under the guise of protesting injustice. What has really been needed in the midst of all the division and chaos is for us as parents to help the next generation find a loving community.

To find community, people must look for the common thread. It might be a hobby like sewing, sports, or animals; it could be music, a language, or a culture. But the strongest common thread in community is a belief system—one that shares the same morals, providing safety and peace to that community. Unfortunately, many who came of age in the 1970s or later have not been raised with an understanding of community. One of the reasons people have tended to turn away from living in community is because many people believe that man is basically evil. Therefore, to avoid evil, and to avoid being hurt, these people who hold this belief stay away from community. People who haven't had a loving community don't understand that it is possible to have a loving community—one that is a safe space without judgement or persecution. This kind of community teaches people that to be a part of it is to pray for wisdom and compassion, to love those around them, and to reach out with kindness. A good community will not only bless others, but also, it will bless the child within.

To best help our children understand the concept of good versus evil, we need to remind them that they are responsible for themselves and their actions. Therefore, they need to be quick to recognize evil when it creeps up on them. One of the ways evil can come in is through manipulating a relationship. In this scenario, one person manipulates another by saying something they don't mean so that the other party feels loved. Then evil continues when the other person has accepted that love, and for that person to prove their love in return, he or she is asked to perform a crime or violence. This scenario is how gangs work. Evil can also come to the surface through disrespect toward elders verbally and physically just because the younger ones think they are smarter and stronger.

> Therefore put on the full armor of God, so that when the day of evil comes, you may be able to stand your ground, and after you have done everything, to stand (Ephesians 6:13 NIV).

In this verse is the reminder to put on the "full armor." Prepare your children for the physical world, which does contain evil and difficulty. In the Book of Isaiah, it says, "What will you do on the day of reckoning (day of evil), when disaster comes from afar? To whom will you run for help? Where will you leave your riches?" (Isaiah 10:3 NIV, text in parenthesis added by the author). The New Living translation expresses this idea in a different way. "What will you do when I punish you, when I send disaster upon you from a distant land? To whom will you turn for help? Where will your treasures be safe?" (Isaiah 10:3 NLT). The day of evil in this verse is a day of punishment. The circumstances of this type of day are not always about actual death and destruction, although the consequences may still be devastating. Some other types of events that may be extreme during this "day" might be a difficult financial or emotional situation like losing your job or failing at a relationship.

This type of "day" could actually be a circumstance where devastation is seen—like when a natural disaster hits. Preparing your child mentally for an emergency, whether personal or otherwise, is one very important part of parenting, and I very seldom meet a student who has been shown how to survive, participate in, and prepare for an emergency. After prayer, safety should be one of the first things we think of when we are preparing our arrow for today's world.

Our world has become a more dangerous place since my childhood. I am sad our children lose their innocence at such a young age, not by choice, but just by observing the world we live in. With billboards, commercials, television shows, books, and everything online, they are robbed of purity before we even get a chance to swoop in and stop the enemy from stealing it.

In addition to helping our children process images we would rather them not see, we need to prepare them to deal with other potential harmful situations and to ensure they know an alternate way to stay connected to us. We taught Lilly her phone number in song at the age of two, knowing that she might need it. Learning how to spell her name also came through song. Both of these bits of information seem small, but they need to be taught as early as possible. My first responder friends say many children who end up in emergency situations do not know their phone number, how to spell their name, or what their parents' names are. Make it a game or song and then keep drilling it until they can do it alone. When Lilly was three, her best friend's mom was bringing her home in the car, and she was running late so she wanted to call me. She didn't think Lilly would know my phone number, but she asked anyway and when Lilly sang it out, she was surprised. Knowing Lilly could recite her name and number, this mom also began to teach her own children this skill.

Your children also need to know where the safe spaces are in the house. Lilly knew that for tornadoes, she was to go straight to the closet under the steps for protection. If there was a fire, she was to shut the door to the room and go through the window to a neighbor's house. As she got older and would stay home alone, we taught her gun safety. She knew where the gun and ammo were (these should never be in the same place for safety reasons). If there was an emergency in which we would be separated, she knew to call (if possible), to tell us her location, and to go to the nearest friend's house. This actually happened during a freak snowstorm. Her carpool could not make it to our house, so they took her to my friend. As she stayed the night there, I had students that I brought home from school, who stayed with me. Don't wait to make a plan. Your children should have a quick response because you have already prepared them for that day.

At fourteen, when Lilly started running up to three miles alone, we gave her a stun gun with a loud alarm. When she began to drive, we had her put the stun gun in her glove box with a laminated card that had the steps of what to do in an accident. Then in her senior year of high school, before she left for Africa, she took self-defense courses. She took first responders first aid and CPR as well. While we raised her to be courteous and mannerly, we also wanted her to be prepared for anything that might be put in her path.

> ...with the belt of truth buckled around your waist...(Ephesians 6:14 NIV).

Honesty is still the best policy when your children ask questions, even when they are about circumstances that are not God-like. Answer these questions. Keep your answers age appropriate, by sharing only the information that answers the questions directly. Don't go on tangents, use visuals, or color outside the lines. Doing so will only muddle up the information. Use scripture to back up your answers. Don't randomly choose a scripture; make sure the verse or passage actually speaks on that topic. This openness and clarity will help build a rapport that will keep the door of communication open.

When you don't know an answer to your children's questions, admit it, and then tell them you will do some research to find the answer. If they are old enough to do the research themselves, have them look up answers online, and then share what they find with you. You still need to do the research yourself because they might have found the information someplace that doesn't have a reputation for truth. Don't correct them if your answer is different, just send them to the website or source where you found the information. Then, let them form their own voice about the topic. If you are honest with them from the beginning, they will return to you over and over when they have questions, even the big ones.

>...with the breastplate of righteousness in place (Ephesians
>6:14 NIV).

Our world suffers from a lack of righteousness, which also means "right thinking." To help your children proverbially place the breastplate of "right thinking" in the midst of a world that doesn't think biblically, teach them the difference between right from wrong. Don't let the world conform their minds to what it considers truth, which is actually only relative truth, or truth according to individuals or groups of people. Only God's Word is the foundational, never-changing truth. Speak His Word to your children and help scripture penetrate and take root in their hearts through repetition. Then show them how to share the truth from the scriptures that are in their hearts with kindness and compassion. Give them the gift of research, so they can weigh any knowledge against the truth of God's Word. Give them tools such as online concordances or commentaries. Ask them to teach you what they learn about God's Word. To this day, I am surprised at what God has taught us through our daughter. She seeks Him, and she shares His truth and love with compassion to those around her.

>...and with your feet fitted with the readiness that comes from
>the gospel of peace (Ephesians 6:15 NIV).

Are we, as parents, ever completely "ready" for any new or difficult situation? Are we comfortable enough with what we have taught our children to let them go to someplace new? Here it says we are "fitted with readiness." I think of the first day of school, when we have scoured the stores to find everything on the list including the perfect backpack to put our children's supplies in. Then the big day comes, and you put your child on the porch for that ever so popular picture. We as parents are nervous, and so are our children. But the excitement overwhelms their fears, and they burst into their first classroom. Until they go to school for the first time, they have basically been sheltered by your thoughts, your plans, and your decisions. When they step out on their own whether at school or in life, it is their turn to be ready.

It is important not to completely shelter your children. Why? They need to know that the world belongs to Satan, and it is filled with evil, yet God did not call us to live in a bubble. He called us to live in the world but not be OF the world. How would we share the Gospel in a bubble? I hear parents who are constantly complaining about what their children should be learning in school. My perspective as a teacher is that life lessons should be taught at home. If you want your child to learn a particular form of literature (the Bible), then read it, out loud, as a family.

If you want your child to learn abstinence, then teach it at home from a biblical worldview, but you have to do it before they are of the age that sexual matters are taught in the schools—which is getting younger and younger! Blaming the schools for teaching your students what that school advertises as its curriculum is not the school's fault. It is your responsibility as the steward of your arrow to educate him or her. This role doesn't mean you have to home school your children. It does mean you have to participate from home and educate your child about what is important to you. Share with them your belief system, your culture, and how you want your family to live life. Without you sharing your knowledge, your child will struggle to have peace. Most kids want to please their parents, but it is hard for the kids when they don't know their parents' thoughts.

In a world of chaos, we cannot rest when we don't know how to find God's peace. Encourage your children to learn how to find the gospel of peace in all situations—even when they face evil in the world. Don't shelter them because that action takes away their opportunity to be ready.

> In addition to all this, take up the shield of faith, with
> which you can extinguish all the flaming arrows of the
> evil one (Ephesians 6:16 NIV).

Did you know your faith is a shield that extinguishes flaming arrows from Satan and his little demons? The faith God is talking about here is the one that replaces fear. When you have the faith of God, fear is not in your vocabulary. In Psalm 23, it says: "I will fear no evil, for you are with me." You can be afraid of evil, but if you have God, there is no reason to fear. Being afraid is actually recognizing the feeling that "fear" is close, and it is time to make a choice about how we respond.

As I've mentioned, fear is a spirit, and that little imp is hard to shake once you have allowed him to hitch a ride. Choose to cast that little imp out by taking those fearful thoughts captive, giving your fears to the Lord, and reminding yourself of His truth. Show your children that it is okay to be afraid, because with the faith of a mustard seed, God will help you overcome that fear as we rely on His Word to find the victory. He is calling us to be conquerors, overcomers, and to be light to the world. In doing so, we set an example that inspires others to also be overcomers, and His peace spreads.

> Take the helmet of salvation…(Ephesians 6:17 NIV).

Taking the helmet of salvation must be our children's choice, not ours. Sharing the reason that you choose Jesus as your Savior is the most important conversation you will ever have with your children. Your life must reflect that you truly trust Him in every situation, seek Him in decisions, and know His Word in a way that you hear it echo in your helmet. Your faith cannot stand in place of your child developing his or her own faith, or he or she will fail. Each person has to put on their own armor, and it starts with the helmet of salvation.

...and the sword of the Spirit, which is the word of God (Ephesians 6:17 NIV).

It is the sword of the Spirit that builds the confidence to fight the good fight. You have to be intentional in teaching God's Word to your children, without slapping them in the face with it. When Lilly was nine, she was asked to read all of Genesis. My husband freaked out a little and quickly said, "I am not sure I want her reading that. Do you know what is in the book of Genesis?" I had the same conversation with other moms. But I knew God would speak to Lilly through those parts that were relevant to her at her age. God is age appropriate. In His Word, she began to see how everyone goes through dark times, and that those times are just part of the journey that makes us cling closer to Jesus. Showing the Bible without the darkness diminishes the importance of the light. We can't hand them the helmet of salvation and then send them out into Satan's playground without the sword of the spirit because Satan is relentless. We need all our armor, and we need to use each piece strategically.

> And pray in the Spirit on all occasions with all kinds of prayers and requests. With this in mind, be alert and always keep on praying for all the Lord's people (Ephesians 6:18 NIV).

Prayer is easy to teach when it is at a meal or bedtime, but how does it fit into the rest of life? In the verse we just read, it says to pray, "...on **all occasions** with all kinds of prayers and requests" (Ephesians 6:18, bold added for emphasis). How do we encourage our children to pray without ceasing, for all situations, good and bad? We show them by our example. We pray, on our knees, in the hurt, during a celebration, through the joblessness, as well as after we get a promotion! We also pray in sickness, or in any situation that comes our way...we pray, daily! We pray during all occasions, giving thanks for everything and everyone who crosses our path. We have to show our children that God answers our prayers, and that He uses our prayers to bring us peace, even if He doesn't answer in the way we plan or want. Sometimes we wait for an answer; sometimes it comes immediately. They need to learn more about how God works, which is sometimes in our timing and sometimes in His.

Teaching your children how to put on the armor of God is the best way to show them how to protect themselves from those unseen forces that work against God. At church, when Lilly was about six, we made up a cheer to put on our armor, and we taught it to all the kids; Lilly knew it well. There are plenty of Ephesians 6 armor pictures on the internet that you can print and post on your home's bathroom mirror to remind your children to put on the armor of God before they start their day. Here is our rendition of the Ephesians 6 cheer:

Armor of God
Puttin' on the armor of God hey, hey
I'm puttin' on the armor of God
So that when the day of evil comes
I can stand my ground.
And after everything He's done, Oh Yeah!
After everything He's done, I'll stand
Stand firm

Puttin' on the armor of God, hey hey
I'm puttin' on the armor of God.

With my belt of truth around my waist
And the breastplate of righteousness now in place
My feet are shod with the Word of God
I'm carrying the Gospel of Peace, oh yeah!
I'm carrying the Gospel of Peace.

Puttin' on the armor of God, hey hey
I'm puttin' on the armor of God

With my shield of faith, there's no debate
Those fiery darts can't penetrate
My helmet of salvation on
The sword of the spirit leads me beyond
On my knees I pray to thee
Lord make me all you want me to be
Because…

I'm puttin' on the armor of God, hey hey
I'm puttin' on the armor of God

Takeaway Transformation Tips for Parenting Our Arrows

- First, we show them His Word and the power found within. #helpthemfindfaith
- Taking the helmet of salvation must be our children's choice, not ours. #helpthemfindfaith
- Your faith cannot stand in place of your child developing his or her own faith, or he or she will fail. #helpthemfindfaith
- It is the sword of the Spirit that builds the confidence to fight the good fight. #helpthemfindfaith
- Showing the Bible without the darkness diminishes the importance of the light. #helpthemfindfaith

Chapter Seventeen

→→→————————————→

A FINAL LOVING WARRIOR WARNING

If you knew I was after the best, why did you do less than the least? (Matthew 25:26b MSG)

The job of parenting is the hardest job we will ever have. We've talked throughout this book about how we are to listen to the Master Warrior so that our children's hearts and minds are trained and focused on His target, not ours. When raising Lilly got difficult, we needed to remind ourselves that the opportunity to be a parent was a gift, and one that the Master Warrior takes quite seriously. He is protective of all His arrows, and He wants each to be cared for in His way.

Although the parable of the talents is widely known and usually associated with gifts or money, I'd like us to apply it to parenting. You will see that God is using the parable as a warning against bad stewardship. But you will also see that the Father rewards those who follow His teaching well for a good outcome. Let's read Matthew 25:24–26 in the Message Bible with the word "child" replacing the one talent.

> "The servant given one **child** said, 'Master, I know you have high standards and hate careless ways, that you demand the best and make no allowances for error. I was afraid I might disappoint you, so I found a good hiding place and secured your **child**. Here it is, safe and sound never **exposed to the world**.'

The master was furious. 'That's a terrible way to live! It's criminal to live cautiously like that! If you knew I was after the best, why did you do less than the least?" (Matthew 25:24–26 MSG, "child" replaces "talent" by this author).

Within this passage, I see two ways in which the Lord could see our parenting skills or the potential lack of care for our children as "criminal" (verse 26). The Lord gives us a warning here that we would be wise to apply to parenting. The first way to not parent is overcautiousness or fear, which is kind of like burying the talent. I meet so many parents who hide their children from the world, keeping them under a rock we call "the Christian bubble" until they are adults. Has your fear of the world caused you to hide your child from knowing the difference between God's love and Satan's deception? By teaching them only a Christian worldview, will they be later deceived by the unknown? We as Christian parents are all tempted to create a bubble, but I ask again, how do you share the Gospel in a bubble? We need to teach our children how to love those in the world without joining them in the world. If we don't, how will that child respond when they leave the safety of your home and their only exposure to the world is what you have let seep in?

The second wrong is that while the Master did not give instructions to the servants about what to do with the talents (Matthew 25:15 MSG), He had been an example of what He expected of the servants, and I am sure they were watching. The servants had a choice as to what they would do with the talents. Their choice would dictate the Master's response, so it was important that they choose wisely. How we rear our children is a choice God gives us, but most of us tend to naturally use the example of our earthly parents rather than intentionally internalizing God's instructions so that we can then pass them on. The Bible is our instruction manual.

Here is how Bill and I applied what we were learning from the parable of the talents. We didn't want to hide Lilly from the world; we wanted to let her explore and be mindful of God's creation while understanding that Satan has corrupted God's purpose for this world. We knew we would have to be investing our time and love in Lilly (our talent), knowing she belongs to the Father (the master). As we look at the servants in the parable of the talents, we were prompted to ask ourselves: Are we the servants who change our lifestyle to sacrifice the material things so that we can give our child the best experience growing up? The answer for us was yes. As I mentioned before, we decided that we would live on one income, so I sold my business to be with Lilly during her developmental years.

For those of you who are single parents, I understand your funds and time are limited, and that your situation is so much more difficult. I still recommend that you find a way to live life with your children. One suggestion might be to find another family to do life with so you can share experiences with their children. We as a family adopted a single mom and her daughter, and we made a way for the daughter to participate in life with us every afternoon while her mom worked. Lilly calls her sister, and they have a wonderful relationship still to this day. Don't feel guilty that you cannot give them everything you want to. What your children want is your time, unhindered by the phone and housework. Do your best to use your time wisely, and God will bless your efforts! I've seen Him take care of single parents!

Who wants to be like the servant who represents the parent who puts their child in a bubble and smothers them in a way that limits their opportunities and experiences because of fear? Or who wants to choose lifestyle over family? At the end of the parable, the words are not kind. The same words apply to parents who bury their children below work and busyness or hide them in the name of protection. There are many parents we have met through the years that fit in with the fearful or greedy servant, and unfortunately, they put themselves in a jail called "regret," because they did not teach their children how to be adults. These parents realize at release time that their kids are not ready for release, and these now grown children either stay at home longer than is ideal or they flounder trying to live on their own.

Chapter Eighteen

TIME TO FLY

The LORD bless you and keep you;
The LORD make his face to shine on you,
and be gracious to you;
The LORD turn his face toward you and give you
peace
(Numbers 6:24–26 NIV).

It is hard to shoot an arrow and fulfill your purpose as a warrior if you don't let go. Crafting the arrow without a planned launch removes its purpose. The arrow will sit wherever it is left, gathering dust in the basement of life. The shaft will begin to lose shape, the feathers will begin to dry rot, and the arrowhead will lose its edge. The purpose of the arrow disappears without being used—and we all need purpose.

Where are they going to GO? Wherever God leads them, but children need to know that you are trusting God enough to release them into the leading of the Holy Spirit. For us, that release included multiple trips, sometimes without us, from the time she was ten through her high school years. Us trusting her to God included signing parental rights to a missionary as God called her at age seventeen to Cape Verde, Africa, for nine months. He later called her to Spain for her first year abroad with Florida State University. God was showing His provision all the way, in every journey. We have to be ready to allow our children the opportunity to know God's calling, and we have to let Him be the wind beneath their wings as they take flight.

During Lilly's sophomore year, we made our last choice with Lilly, which was what to do after she graduated. When Lilly was eleven, we had taken her on a mission trip to Germany. Knowing she would graduate at seventeen, her father and I suggested she take a gap year before she attended college. We then made a plan to travel the world together as a family, during which time we would visit all our missionary friends throughout the year, but God had other plans. During Lilly's junior year, our missionary friends were all returning to the states with no plans of going back.

Lilly began to pray about what she should do as a gap year. She chose a program called Global Year based in Woodstock, Georgia, although the organization sends students all over the world. This would be a nine-month commitment, living in a foreign country, learning the language, possibly working for an orphanage, or teaching English at a preschool, and ministering to the community in which the students lived. After her acceptance, she chose the Dominican Republic, and she was excited about serving the needs of a missionary couple, but in late March, things began to change. After a meeting with Global Year, she came home and explained that the couple had returned to the states for medical reasons. They gave her a couple of choices as to where she could go, and she landed on Cape Verde. Where is Cape Verde?

My husband, needless to say, was a little nervous...and disappointed. He had already made plans with pilot friends to be able to send packages to the Dominican Republic for Lilly and was looking forward to the visit. We began to scour the internet for information about Cape Verde, a little group of islands in the Atlantic, and there were no videos except one by the Mormons. We found very little detail about crime, culture, and housing. But, as her parents, we needed God's confidence, and we needed to support what God had put on her heart. God proved his plan—He provided every last dime of the $14,500 she needed to raise, to go. It was hard to make the decision to let go, signing away our parental rights, and allowing God to be solely in control. We were both hesitant, and the realization was difficult that we were closing a chapter, moving into serving more as mentors than parents to Lilly.

Lilly's experiences in Cape Verde helped her embrace God's love and compassion for people in need. Since she has been back in the U.S., as mentioned before, she has carried single dollar bills and bottles of water in her car to give to those who might need them. She also sometimes has new socks, personal hygiene items, gloves, or hats. When she arrived at college, she made sure she knew where the organizations and churches were that would help those she sees in need. From her, we have learned how to respond to the needs of those around us. Through her, God has shared with us that even the smallest act of kindness can help someone who is soul searching respond to His call. What we have learned from Lilly's generosity has become our new normal when it comes to helping others. Her response to those in need has shown us that it is important to remember that as parents, you are shaping the arrowhead of your arrow to ultimately, at release, penetrate the world for God.

Takeaway Transformation Tips for Parenting Our Arrows

- It is hard to shoot an arrow and fulfill your purpose as a warrior if you don't let go. #beawarrior
- Children need to know that you are trusting God enough to release them into the leading of the Holy Spirit. #helpthemfindfaith
- We have to be ready to allow our children the opportunity to know God's calling, and we have to let Him be the wind beneath their wings as they take flight. #helpthemfindflight
- The realization was difficult as we were closing a chapter and moving into serving more as mentors than parents to our child. #helpthemfindflight
- Remember that as parents, you are shaping the arrowhead of your arrow to ultimately, at release, penetrate the world for God. #bethewarrior

Chapter Nineteen

FROM QUIVER TO *HIS* TARGET

He has made My mouth like a sharp sword,
In the shadow of His hand He has kept Me hidden;
And He has made Me a sharpened arrow,
In His quiver He has hidden Me (Isaiah 49:2 AMP).

Bill and I did know that Lilly was ready for release, but we still did our best to get in a few more lessons as that day approached. As I mentioned, Lilly took a self-defense class. We also had a garage sale so she could earn those last few traveling dollars. She learned how to pack nine months into one backpack, and we helped her organize paperwork and passports. It was so rewarding to watch Lilly be excited for the next chapter of her life.

Lilly was ready to make the big, life-changing decisions because we gave her choices in the littler ones. She understood there were good and bad consequences to her decisions. She knew she would make many mistakes. She learned how to seek God's target for her before it was time for her first launch. When it came to her launch day, we knew she was ready for release.

She trusted God before she got there because He proved Himself over and over to her while she still lived under the cover of our family. God was her Provider because she had seen Him provide—not just for our family daily, but for His calling for her to go to Praia, Cape Verde. As I have said, but it's worth repeating: every cent, including spending money, was provided. God was her healer of the hurt she felt when many of her friends called her crazy for choosing Africa for nine months over college. But God proved her friends wrong when He met her in Africa and Lilly saw Him move. God showed her she could learn their language, which gave her more opportunities to minister to the native people. She also missed playing soccer, and she wanted to help the churches create a soccer program for the children in the daycares and communities. God answered her prayer by introducing her to a professional female soccer player from Brazil who was looking for someone to help her set up programs throughout the island. The church connected them. While Lilly was in Africa, she saw people's lives changed. Many were baptized, and many families were united in marriage within the Cape Veridian culture where they do not normally marry.

One of the hardest parts of life is letting those we love take their own journeys. I want to end this book with the best outcome of how our arrow hit her target: Lilly had chosen God for herself. She was not riding on our coattails of belief—she owned her own coattails, and she wore them with joy. We watched in awe of what God had done during the previous seventeen years. We are so thankful for His Holy Spirit, who had shown us so many ways in which to help her grow into the young woman of God standing before us. The last night before her flight, we did our usual goodnight banter of who loves who more, and she gave us her usual closing response of "That's enough, we win." Boy, did we!

Takeaway Transformation Tips for Parenting Our Arrows

- One of the hardest parts of life is letting those we love take their own journey. #helpthemfindflight

To Know Jesus

To know Jesus is to know His love. And to know His love is to have the love you need to love your children. That love, no matter what the circumstance, will surpass all understanding because we are to love as God loves us. His love is unconditional. Every time you commit a sin against someone or yourself, you sin against God because He created you and those around you. God sent His Son to die on a cross so that you would not have to carry that sin any longer.

It is hard to believe that God would do something so extravagant and sacrificial for us when we are so prone to sin against Him. It's because of this sacrifice of having His Son die that you can believe God loves you! He is not talking about the surface, "here today, gone tomorrow," way that the world loves. John 1:1 says, "In the beginning was the Word and the Word was with God and the Word was God." That means that Jesus, His only Son, was with God when this world was created. He wasn't just with God; they were designing you, who you would be, and what your purpose would be on Earth.

The greatest gift that we can give our children is sharing the love of Christ. If you do not know that Jesus died for you on a cross so that you could be forgiven of your sin to reconnect with the God who created you, this is your opportunity. God loves you. All you have to do is confess with your mouth that Jesus died on the cross for your sins, went to the depths of hell to retrieve the keys of life, and rose again to sit at the right hand of his Father—our eternal Father—God. This confession is said in faith. You are not saved by your good deeds; only faith brings salvation to your soul for eternity. You are not saved by theology; you are not saved by intellect. You are saved one hundred percent with faith. No cost, no work—just faith. So, if you want to ask Jesus to be the Savior of your life, say this short prayer with me.

Dear Jesus, I recognize that You are the Savior of the world. I understand that God sent You here so that you could take my sin on the cross and die in my place. I know that Your blood was spilled, not mine. It is because of You that I can be reunited with our Father. I believe that You were crucified, died, and was buried. On the third day, You arose, and You walked this earth for forty days. During that time, You revealed Yourself to five hundred people who saw Your face and Your scars of the crucifixion. You spoke with them to prepare them for Your Holy Spirit. Jesus, I hand You my life, my heart, and my mind. Take it that I might reside with You for eternity. In Jesus' name, I pray. AMEN!

Now that you have come to know Jesus as your Lord and Savior, a relationship begins. It's time to get to know Him. Please open your Bible to the Gospel of John and begin to read so that you may begin to know your Savior. Your new relationship with Him will help you build the relationship with your children. To grow and mature in your faith, you will need a spiritual family to help hold you accountable and share in the wisdom that you will glean from your daily time with Jesus. Look for a local church that will edify your soul and speak only the words of truth from God's Word—the Bible. May God bless you and keep you as you steward your arrow.

About the Author

Tammy Largin is a wife, mother, debut author, speaker, and lifelong teacher, loving life in Jacksonville, Florida, with her husband, Bill, and their dog Roxi. As their daughter, Lilly blossoms in adulthood, Tammy's heart is full seeing God's goodness and the fruits of biblical parenthood.

During the last thirty-eight years, Tammy has poured into the lives of other people's children as she served as a teacher educating them on multiple subjects from the art of being an equestrian, to dance, to American Sign Language, to history, and to a multitude of other educational topics. Living life as a teacher has allowed her to invest in students of all ages, challenging them to live a life of service and truth.

Tammy is a bit of a dare angel. She is an adventure seeker who loves the beautiful experiences the outdoors hold, including rafting down the Colorado and the Ocoee Rivers, mountain biking or climbing mountains, jumping horses over fences, or taking a dive from a perfectly good airplane.

Tammy believes life is a journey given to us by God to be lived well with no regrets yet, she recognizes the value found in regret once it is embraced. Healing can come from that which cannot be changed; eventually becoming a testimony of God's unending grace. She encourages others to lean into every learning opportunity because God's Word says, "For the Lord gives wisdom; from his mouth come knowledge and understanding;" (Proverbs 2:6 ESV). Her dad once told her that knowledge is the only thing that can't be taken away from you, so let us just say she collects it.

Tammy intentionally asks thought-provoking questions of all believers, challenging them to look outside of themselves and their own lives. She asks them to reflect, evaluate who they are, and what does life look like through her questioning: *Are we taking advantage of the time we have on Earth to really live life to its fullest the way God intended? Are we enjoying life like He would have us do in the Garden, living with less, loving people, watching nature, and sharing the freedom found in His Son? Or are we living in fear, poverty of spirit, and participating in the rat race of the world ignoring the beautiful life God has given us?*

Tammy hopes these questions will help sharpen the body of Christ so that each member is a weapon worthy of being wielded in the Lord's hands to make an impact for the Kingdom. She believes strongly in living in communion so that she can both sharpen and be sharpened, as God instructs us in the following verse: "As iron sharpens iron, so one person sharpens another" (Proverbs 27:17 NIV).

Acknowledgements

First and foremost, I want to thank God, my Father, whose creativity He has shared with me and my husband as we raised our beautiful arrow. To know Jesus is to know love, joy, and peace in the midst of parenthood.

To my husband, Bill, for all his love and support as we raised our daughter together, sharing ideas that God provided so that our daughter would have a heart for God's calling. What a wonderful life we share with Jesus.

To my beautiful Lilly, your desire to please God and press on toward His goal, even when you are afraid, gives courage to all of us who watch Him use you in so many ways. The love you have for those around you is contagious and God uses you to share that love all over the world.

To my momma and my dad, what a wonderful life I have lived because of your bravery to share experiences with me that I carried over to raising our daughter. I love you both dearly.

Thank you to my family and friends, who have said multiple times that I need to write this book. Thank you for the inquiries and holding me accountable during my writing season. Thank you for your input and prayers that kept me seeking truth on parenting in God's Word.

To my pastor, Joby Martin at Church of Eleven22, your insight into scripture has challenged me to dig deeper into God's wisdom everyday as I read His Word. Your willingness to speak truth from the pulpit without apology, yet with compassion, has sparked in me a desire to share the wisdom God has shared with me so that others can know Christ and the freedom He provides in a world full of chains.

Thank you to the men and women at Southern Georgia Traditional Archery and Primitive Skills Club and Northern Georgia Traditional

Archery for their time and patience as I asked so many questions about traditional bow and arrow crafting. You gave me clarity as I sought God about why He calls our children arrows.

Thank you to Loral Pepoon, my editor and publisher, who repeatedly brought me back from the rabbit trail so God could use me to convey His message of biblical parenting.

Thank you to my friend Kelle Mac from Kelle Mac Photogaphy for making me look so beautiful.

To the Warrior Writers, my sisters in Christ, who have not only poured into me, but encouraged me to dig deeper into God's Word for more as He revealed His truth in parenting. I could not have made it to the finish line without you and your prayers.

A very special thank you to Missy Maxwell Worton. Without your coming alongside me through this process, I would have been lost. God has created you for such a time as this, and He is using you to help so many of us share our stories through healed hearts for Kingdom purpose.

Notes

1. *Merriam Webster*, s.v. "dedicate (v.)", accessed April 20, 2023, https://www.merriam-webster.com/dictionary/dedicate.

2. *Blue Letter Bible*, s.v. "qānâ" (H7069) Strong's Hebrew lexicon (NIV), accessed February 27, 2024, https://www.blueletterbible.org/lexicon/h7069/niv/wlc/0-1/

3. *Blue Letter Bible*, s.v. "yārē" (H3372) Strong's Hebrew Lexicon (NIV), accessed February 27, 2024, https://www.blueletterbible.org/lexicon/h3372/niv/wlc/0-1/

4. *Blue Letter Bible*, s.v "pālâ" (H6395)Strong's Hebrew Lexicon (NIV), accessed February 27,2024, https://www.blueletterbible.org/lexicon/h6395/niv/wlc/0-1/

5. *Oxford Learners Dictionary,* s.v. "wonder (n.)," accessed February 27, 2024, https://www.oxfordlearnersdictionaries.com/definition/english/wonder_2.

6. "Baby Carrier, Sling or Wrap: Which Should You Choose?" *CNET*, accessed October 31, 2023, www.cnet.com/health/parenting/baby-carrier-sling-or-wrap-which-should-you-choose/.

7. *Metagenics Blog,* "How Screens are Altering the Landscape of the Brain. Metagenics Blog," last modified April 17, 2019, accessed March 25, 2023,

https://blog.metagenics.com/post/2019/04/26/how-screens-are-altering-the-landscape-of-the-brain/.

8.   Joby Martin (Host), "Anything Is Possible: Do You Believe Even When Doubts Creep In?" *Deepen*, Audio podcast episode: May 8, 2023, S07E05, The Church of Eleven22, https://youtu.be/z7X8th1AFwY,accessed January 12, 2024.

9.   Bruce Frank, "Saturated, Night 3," Sermon at Church of Eleven 22, Jacksonville, Florida, September 16, 2022.

10. "Ten Commandments List," Bibleinfo.Com, www.bibleinfo.com/en/topics/ten-commandments-list, accessed October 31,2023.

11. Thomas Hines, *The Rise and Fall of the American Teenager* (Harper Perennial; Reprint edition (September 19, 2000).

12. Jon Savage, *Teenager: The Creation of Youth Culture* (Pimlico, 2008).

13. Joby Martin, "Thy Kingdom Come," Sermon at The Church of Eleven22, Jacksonville, Florida, January 23, 2022.

Book Suggestions

The Five Love Languages by Gary Chapman

The Five Love Languages Test
https://pd.santarosa.edu/sites/pd.santarosa.edu/files/lovelanguagetest.pdf

Anything is Possible by Joby Martin and Charles Martin

Personality Plus by Florence Littinaur

The Treasure Tree by John Trent and Gary Smalley

Chicken Fingers, Mac and Cheese...Why Do You Always Have To Say Please by Wendy Rosen and Jackie End

Heritage Research Information

- Ancestry.com (use at the library for free or subscription)
- FamilySearch.org (free)

Printed in the USA
CPSIA information can be obtained
at www.ICGtesting.com
LVHW052145300924
792574LV00002B/5